KW-459-285

MORE THAN A VOYAGE

Stories of Voyaging in Ireland,
Cornwall and Brittany

John O'Connor

Illustrations by Barry Curtin

ORIGINAL WRITING

ISBNS
PARENT : 978-1-78237-781-8
EPUB: 978-1-78237-787-0
MOBI: 978-1-78237-788-7
PDF: 978-1-78237-789-4

A CIP catalogue for this book is available from the National Library.
Published by ORIGINAL WRITING LTD., Dublin, 2014.
Printed and Bound by Berforts Information Press, Stevenage.

For Family

In two continents

Acknowledgments

Many thanks to:

Fr Gearoid O Donnchadha for allowing me access to his – much prized, I'm sure – logbook for *An tSiochain* and for expressing great interest in, and support for, my undertaking.

Barry Curtin, who always said, 'No problem', when I demanded illustrations, often at short notice. This book is better for his gifts.

Seamus O'Donoghue, world sailor, who helped with dates and personnel regarding the voyages of *Second Wind*.

Numerous family and friends who encouraged and regularly enquired as to the progress of this work.

The teams at Original Writing and Carrowmore Publishing Consultancy.

Contents

Part Two
Polyanna

Part Three
Eibhlís

Foreword

For a thousand generations the Atlantic Ocean has fascinated those who dwell on the 'far shores of civilisation': the Sumerians, the Egyptians, the Greeks, the Romans and the Irish. In the words of the song, *'it tore men's boats asunder but it gave men dreams to dream'*. The wide ocean has always been a challenge and a dream. We find it so in the *Arabian Nights*, in *Sinbad the Sailor*, and in *Aesop's Fables*, which were probably the source of the whale and other stories associated with Saint Brendan and his travels. Thomas Merton summed up the attitude of Brendan and the host of Irish seafarers:

We are exiles in the far end of solitude, living as listeners,
With hearts attending to the skies we cannot understand:
Waiting upon the first far drums of Christ the Conqueror,
Planted like sentinels upon the world's frontier.

John O'Connor is, like Brendan, a Kerryman from Dingle, on the farthest west coast of Europe. Like Brendan, John has always been fascinated by the sea. For his profession he chose boatbuilding, which he taught for many years in the Institute of Technology in Tralee (ITT). He built several sailing dinghies, dreaming all the while of the challenges of the sea and landfalls in far-off places. This book makes available to the amateur and to the professional some of the adventures John encountered during his eventful life.

I met John when I took up a teaching position in the ITT in 1980. I had been teaching in New York for many years and came home across the Atlantic in *An tSiochâin*, a 41-foot Bounty class fibreglass sailing boat. John was interested in the boat and in my journey. We found we shared many of the same interests and quickly became friends. John was a great resource and companion. We shared many voyages together, some of which John has recounted. John is an accomplished singer and guitar player. Memorable was his rendering of 'Dingle Bay' as we passed the headlands of Cornwall, Brittany and Scotland.

In fair and foul weather, John was a resourceful crewmate to whom I am sincerely grateful.

Gearoid O Donnchadha

Introduction

A voyage is described as a journey, especially a long journey by sea; it is also described as a journey to an unknown place. This latter description is probably the most accurate as the word truly evokes not only the adventure of travel, but the uncertainty and wonders that await one at the end of a voyage. In the early days of my voyaging when I was heading for new places, that sense of wonder and anticipation was always there and to this day I still enjoy setting off and dropping my anchor in a new harbour.

This book is the result of my experiences with the crews who sailed with me over the years and the numerous people who welcomed us ashore. It is for all of those people who fill the pages to follow, the ones with a richness of spirit and wit and a welcoming way, the ones who opened their doors to a voyager.

I chose the title *More Than a Voyage* because the journeys described herein were always more than a journey from one set of co-ordinates to another. They were peopled by a wide range of characters, young and old; the green and the wise lumped together into a crew with a common focus. Each journey was different in its wider scope and in the personal satisfaction it brought to individual crew members.

Arriving at the other end *is* important, but it is what happens between departure and landfall that makes the journey, and that is more than a voyage.

John O'Connor

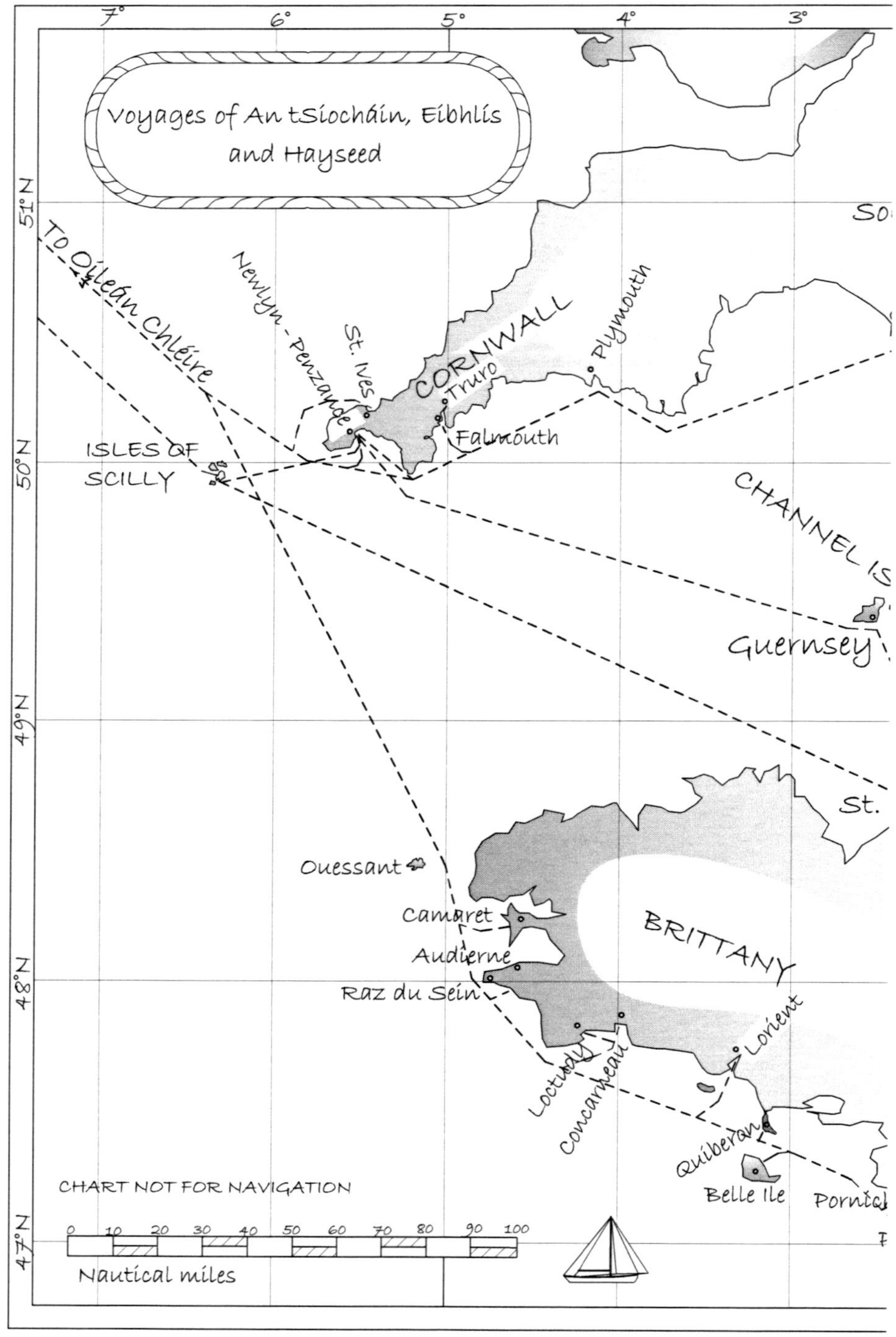

Voyages of An tSiocháin, Eibhlís and Hayseed
7°
6°
5°
4°
3°
51°N
50°N
49°N
48°N
47°N
To Oileán Chléire
Newlyn - Penzance
St. Ives
CORNWALL
Truro
Plymouth
Falmouth
ISLES OF SCILLY
CHANNEL IS
Guernsey
St.
Ouessant
Camaret
Audierne
Raz du Sein
BRITTANY
Lorient
Loctudy
Concarneau
Quiberon
Belle Ile
Pornic
CHART NOT FOR NAVIGATION
0 10 20 30 40 50 60 70 80 90 100
Nautical miles

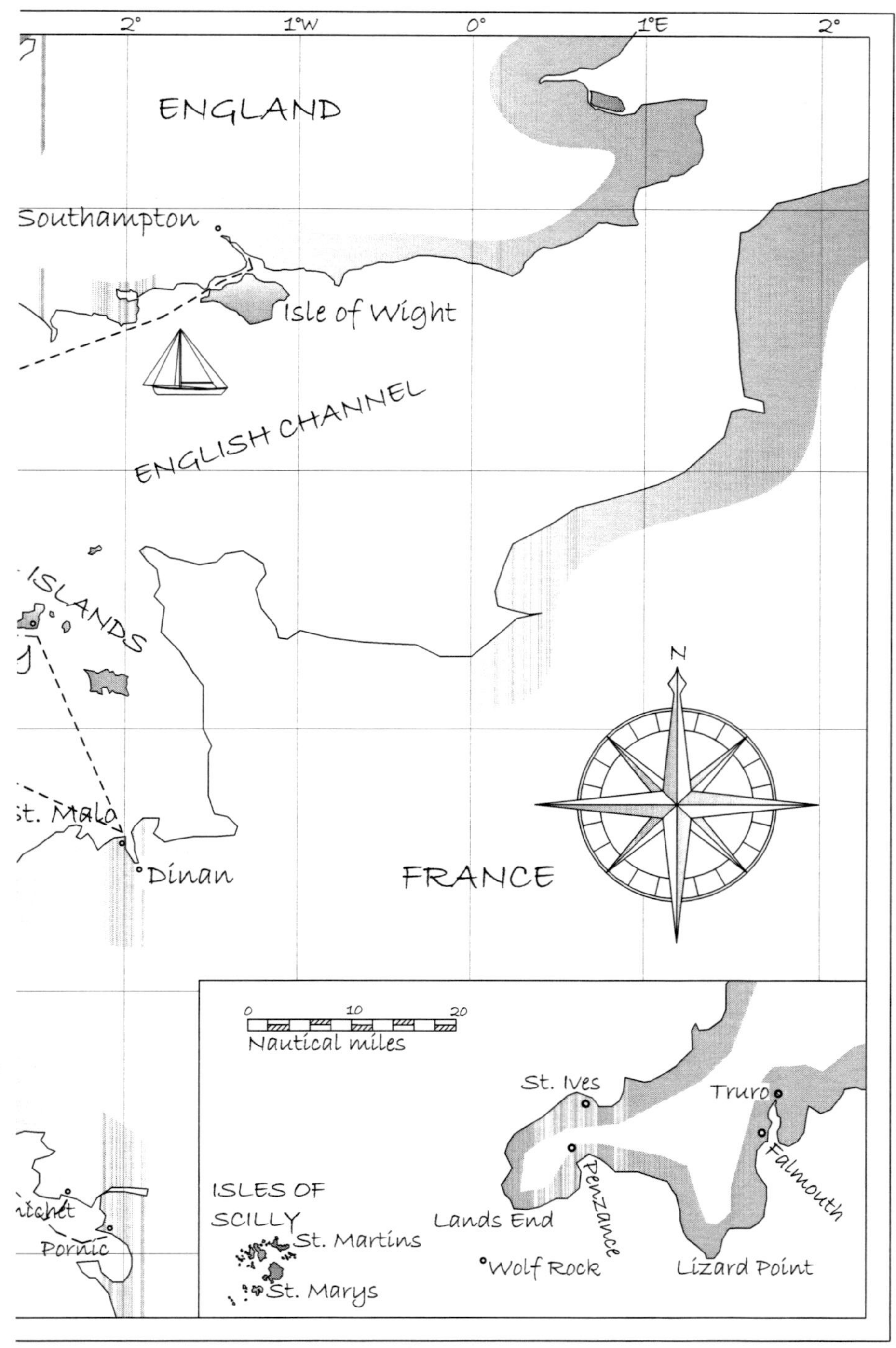
2°
1°W
0°
1°E
2°
ENGLAND
Southampton
Isle of Wight
ENGLISH CHANNEL
ISLANDS
St. Malo
Dinan
FRANCE
N
0
10
20
Nautical miles
St. Ives
Truro
Falmouth
Penzance
ISLES OF SCILLY
St. Martins
St. Marys
Lands End
Wolf Rock
Lizard Point
Pornic

Part One

An tSiocháin

Chapter 1

A Stroll Round the Deck

The stem of *An tSiochâin* pummelled the angry sea as we approached Mizen Head from the north under a grey mist-sodden cloak. The wind shrieked constantly without catching its breath for the briefest respite. The boat was surging ahead, steady on her course and confident in her task as she answered to the controls manned by Fr Gearoid in the cockpit. He held the wheel firmly; his stance, practised and perfected during many years sailing, was anchored to the cockpit sole and gave no hint of the internal stresses at work in his legs and lower body. His gaze was fixed on the sea ahead and his eyes glinted with a mixture of caution and thrill. This was his thing: his hobby, his challenge, his oneness with the elements. Sailors bring differing things to the sea and take from it experiences which are varied and wondrous according to their individual perceptions. Fr Gearoid enjoyed going to sea in a sailing boat with good company and sharing the wonder of the experience with the crew; the deeper satisfaction it brought his inner self was his alone to understand. Some sailors like to sail competitively in racing yachts; many more use the vehicle as a showpiece to impress; and others see the boat as a mode of conveyance to different ports where various onshore enjoyments are on offer when they disembark. For Gearoid it was primarily about the voyage and the opportunities it presented to pass on a love of sailing to his charges.

With the Mizen on our port beam, *An tSiochâin* was ploughing through a rough sea tossed by windswept waves; her prow was now dipping into the crests that struck the bow at an oblique angle from the south-west. A foresail that was lashed in storage to the starboard guard rail had come loose and was being whipped about by the wind and washed with vigour by the waves each time the bow slammed down into the oncoming sea. Gearoid, who was occupied at the wheel holding the sleek eight and a half-ton yacht on course, asked Seán Gannon, a friend of Gearoid's with whom I was sailing for the first time, to take the helm while he and I went forward to tie down the sail lest it be lost to the sea.

We clipped on and made our way forward through the lashing rain and whistling wind. From time to time the bow would lurch downward and throw the sea to one side. As we approached the bow we knelt on the deck and crawled the final metre. Gearoid gathered in the sail in gwalls, which fought him at every turn, while I tied it down as the lashing line whipped me about the face like I was a recalcitrant schoolboy in a Dickens novel. Every thirty seconds a larger wave would come and swamp us to the waist and we had to shout above the wind to communicate. After an exhausting ten minutes we had accomplished our task, which in retrospect was like wrestling a wild white stallion whose limbs and mane were flailing about in an effort to avoid being bedded down. We returned to the cockpit and slumped down on to the seat beside Seán, who was standing erect and determinedly trying to hold the course. He was livid that he had been left alone in the cockpit and not made privy to the shenanigans of his two crewmates on the foredeck. 'What were ye doing up front for so long?' he inquired of me. I looked at Gearoid, who was enjoying his rest on the seat opposite. 'You didn't notice?' I answered. 'We just decided to take a leisurely stroll around the foredeck.' It's a story Gearoid loves to tell and I know he will delight in having it included here. After rounding the Mizen we made east for the sheltered and hospitable north harbour in Oileán Chléire.

Seán Gannon was great and easy company; a soft-spoken gentleman whom I remember smiled with his eyes. I was delighted to meet him again several years later when he docked in Dingle with his own boat in the company of Gearoid. I was glad to be in a position at the time to render them assistance as their vessel was having some minor engine problems. During their stay Gearoid asked if I would go on a short trip in the harbour with them before they departed; he wanted to have the three of us on board again in memory of the cruise when he and I walked the foredeck for want of something better to do. I obliged with pleasure and we had a happy and jolly hour reminiscing about times past. Before they sailed out of the harbour to continue their voyage, they left behind a gift to thank me for the assistance I had given them; it was gift enough sailing in their company again.

Battle with foresail

Chapter 2

BEGINNINGS

In 1980 *An tSiocháin* sailed into Ballydavid Harbour in the Dingle peninsula after thirty days crossing the Atlantic from New York. On board was a man with whom I would spend many hours at sea over the following ten years. Fr Gearoid O Donnchadha, the owner of the boat, was coming home to take up a position in Tralee Regional Technical College (now the Institute of Technology Tralee) as a lecturer in sociology. I was already employed in the college, teaching apprenticeship shipwright students; that is where our paths crossed, Gearoid's and mine. Joe Motherway, a mutual colleague, introduced me to Gearoid after he took up his position in the college. Joe knew that Gearoid and I would have things in common in view of our association with boats. Joe would subsequently sail with us and adopted the role of ship engineer; his skills included engine maintenance and he gave of his time freely to *An tSiocháin*, ensuring that she was fit for voyaging. The yacht that brought Gearoid eastward from New York to Ballydavid was a Philip Rhodes-designed Bounty II, one of the world's first fibreglass production yachts, a noble and robustly built vessel, forty foot in length with a long keel ballasted soundly to handle her large sail area; in heavy weather she sailed as if a furrow was laid out in front of her to dig into. Her hull was thick with layers of glass and resin unlike the GRP boats that followed in later years; one could not but have confidence that she would always see you home safely. She was a supremely comfortable cruising yacht.

It was on *An tSiocháin* that I was introduced to yacht sailing and navigation. I was invited along by Gearoid initially to crew with himself and Joe and other colleagues from the college on trips in Tralee bay. Kay Fitzgerald was a regular on some of the shorter trips. Later I accompanied Gearoid on several cruises which would bring us far from *An tSiocháin's* home port of Fenit. Fr Gearoid's knowledge of yacht sailing was considerable at this juncture while my experience was sufficient for inshore dinghy boating. My knowledge of boats and their construction in general was well founded as I had served my apprenticeship as a shipwright before going back to college and becoming a teacher.

And so began my initiation into the world of big boat sailing, navigation and seamanship under the tutelage of a well-found practitioner of the art. Gearoid and I shared mutual respect. We both brought different skills to the partnership: my background in boatbuilding married well with Gearoid's pastime. I would deal with any construction and repair issues while Gearoid dealt with the responsibility of voyage preparation and execution. It wasn't long before we fell into an easy relationship of equals and that eventually led to a good friendship that endures to this day.

But it wasn't all plain sailing; put a handful of people on a boat for a couple of weeks and the confinement in close quarters will lead to irksome behaviour by the most passive of souls. In most of the voyages on *An tSiochåin* there would be four or five on board, and the cruises took in various ports on the coast of Ireland, Cornwall in England and Brittany in France.

I learned about navigation in a time before global positioning systems, commonly known as GPS. A trailing log over the stern clocked up our speed through the water and distance travelled. This information had to be further analysed and adjusted for tidal streams and leeway of the ship through the water. A position was then marked on the chart and any necessary course correction was implemented. After a time Gearoid left the navigation in my hands and by and large we always ended up where we were supposed to be.

Fr Gearoid said mass on the boat every day when at sea and was happy that the crew participated out of their own volition. We all willingly took part, shared the readings and the wine cup in the middle of the sea; there was something special in the ceremony in that setting that encouraged participation. Gearoid told me of when he was sailing across the Atlantic and how the mass became a high point of the day.

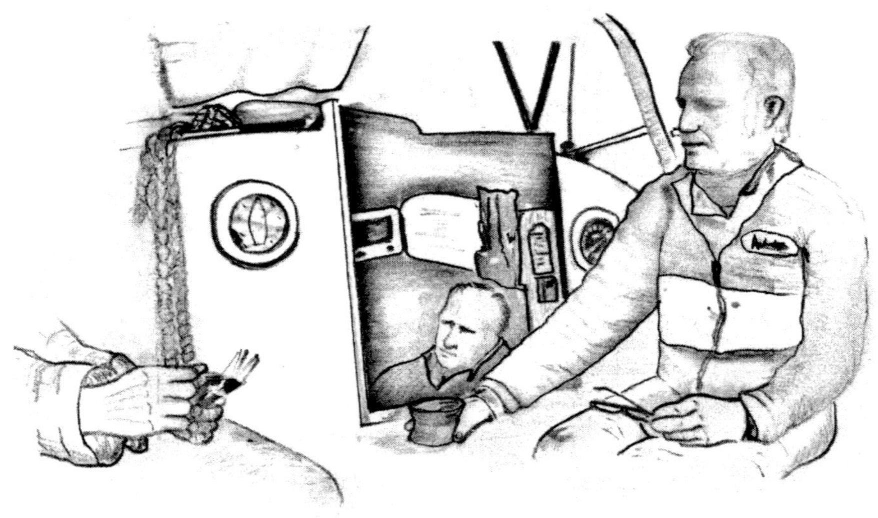

Mass onboard: Fr. Gearóid, right; Jim Drennon down below; Author, left, reading.

One day in a storm when he was in the throes of seasickness and didn't want to leave his bunk, Bill Verity, a legend of the sea who was skippering *An tSiochháin* across the Atlantic came looking for him and told him that the men were waiting on deck for the mass. He couldn't but rally himself and say the mass in the face of such an appeal.

In latitudes between 47° 07'N and 53° 37'N, in a series of voyages, our crew would celebrate mass each day under sun, wind or rain, far from the trappings of marble and silver iconography or lofty stained-glass windows, which modern mass-goers expect to accompany the service. It occurs to me now that we crew were like the apostles of old who celebrated mass in similar simplicity.

Chapter 3

Good Company

Sailors often debate how time appears to pass unnoticed while at sea; on coastal trips the passing of headlands is an event and the distance between some can be several hours, yet the time in between, whether filled with stories, song or banter, or indeed with contemplation or reading, can pass completely unnoticed. This reinforces my belief that the undertaking is indeed about the journey. Looking back, the journeys merge into one and I cannot remember which story came from which journey. All I know is that they came from a particular boat and its family at the time (in this case that of *An tSiochâin*), but that doesn't matter to me. My recollections are not diminished in any way if they are in disarray in my mind; all that is paramount is that they are there, that in the past there was a time of joy and fun and companionship that registered in my consciousness as a time to be remembered in the future.

Gearoid and I were having a chat one day apart from the rest of the crew and the topic was carpentry. He often complimented me on my skills in that area and that day he was linking me with St Joseph and Jesus, who had the same trade. 'I wonder what kind of a chippy He was,' I offered. The discussion veered lightly into the comparative carpentry skills of the Galilean and me; it was an exchange that started innocuously and grew into humorous banter. I may have inquired as to the duration of an apprenticeship in those days and if He had to pay to learn the trade, as was common in the not too distant past. Back and forth it went and I eventually decided to go for the punchline: 'He may have been a good carpenter,' I said, 'but He never made L1.' (At the time, L1 described my teaching grade at Tralee RTC.) Gearoid took the punchline with aplomb and smiled.

When sailing close to the wind with stories to a priest there is always a line of demarcation in your mind which you are trying to gauge based on how well you know the man of the cloth. Another time we were exchanging limericks and it came to my turn:

There was a young lady from Madras

(And I heard from the helm, 'Hang on, hang on now'. I continued.)

She stood in water up to her knees
That will rhyme when the tide comes in.

That time I couldn't quite gauge Gearoid's response at the completion of the verse; perhaps it was too close to the wind.

Gearoid presented himself as a man-of-the-world type of guy on the one hand and on the other his devoutness was evident. On meeting him for the first time, there is nothing to indicate his vocation and with such undefinable signals, some, on the first encounter, can trip up in the vocabulary stakes. It took me some time to get used to the idea that I was in the presence of a non-lay person. It is not that I was a frequent user of bad language – I actually cannot abide it – but there are areas of lay living that one can stray into describing with one's peers, descriptions that need a certain softness when within earshot of a priest. For instance, I brought a friend on board *An tSiocháin* who wasn't aware of the situation. He was dropping his bag onto the deck of the boat, but it missed and ended up in the water. 'Jesus,' he exclaimed. Gearoid was nearby and he leaned toward my mate and said 'Friend of yours?'

Although he was an ordained priest, he also understood that the crew were of a different leaning and in his own way he respected our condition and accepted our failings with good spirit. We all respected him for his abilities aboard the boat as well as feeling that respect which was due to him by virtue of his vocation. He must have been considered strange by many (though never by me) because of his apparently non-clerical attitude. He could be found ripping the guts out of a ship's head (toilet) at three o'clock in the morning in the middle of a voyage or climbing to the masthead to free a tangled halyard in a rolling sea. His attire was like my own: deck shoes, denims and t-shirt. He liked to hear songs sung on the trips and a favourite of his went:

And what's it to any man whether or no,
whether I'm easy or whether I'm true
As I lifted her petticoat easy and slow,
and I rolled up my sleeve for to buckle her shoe.

Gearoid liked good company and the crew during my years sailing with him was always varied and interesting; he seemed to get a cross section of people who fitted well with one another. His nieces and nephews joined him frequently, as did mutual colleagues from the college. Len Breewood, naval architect, mechanical engineer, aficionado of good food and ship's barber, crewed with us on a couple of cruises to Cornwall and Brittany.

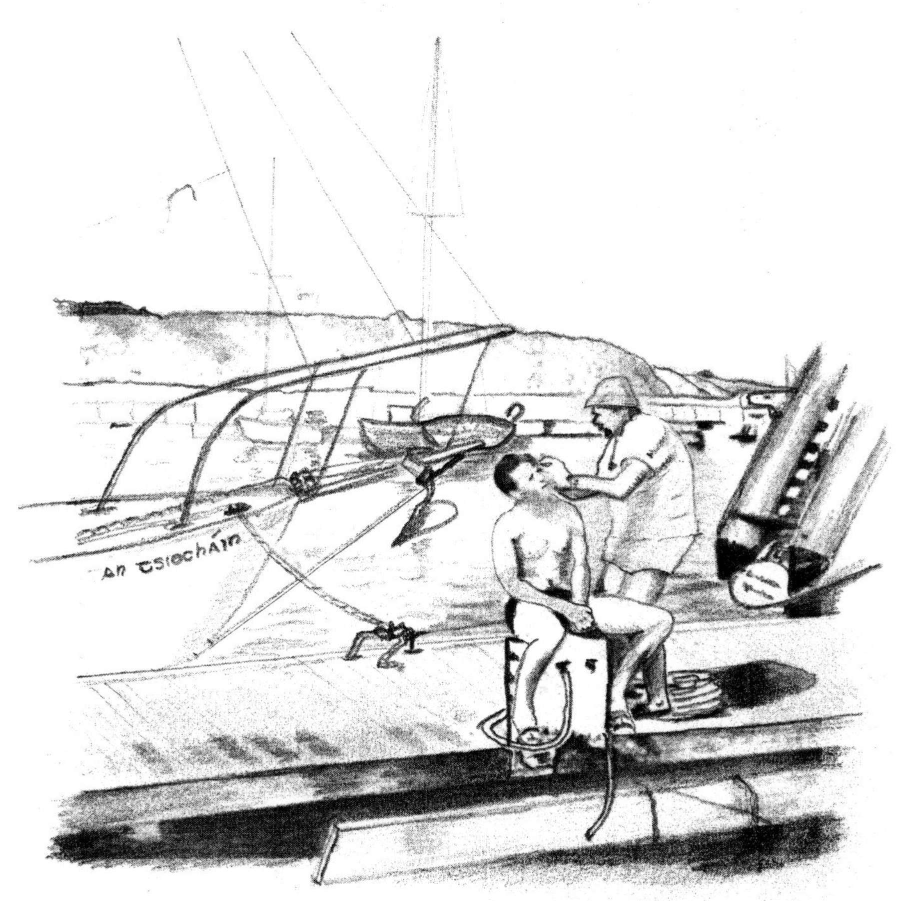

Len giving Riobárd a haircut

Len was a colourful character with a good sense of humour; he liked a good yarn with regular company as much as dressing up in his uniform for a buffet with 'Coiste an Asgard'. Len was a director of The Irish

Sail Training Association for several years and had he still been with us when *Asgard II*, that noble ship which represented our sea heritage and boatbuilding skills, went down in the Bay of Biscay in 2008, he would have felt its loss deeply.

He loved to cook and on the cruises he automatically assumed the role of provider for the crew. He used to strap himself in front of the gimballed galley cooker when the boat was heeled and produced several good meals at various angles of heel. Len specialised in sauces and I can remember looking to the galley and seeing him dollop white wine over the giddy pan while stirring; the odd swig would also find its way to Len's mouth and I would call down and ask: 'Need any help there Len?' Gearoid enquired of me once while Len was in the midst of a swirl aromatic steam as the cooker was horizontal, Len vertical and the mast at an angle of fifty degrees, 'Is he alright down there, John?'

After the meal on board, Gearoid was always keen to do the wash-up right away after eating; this was usually done in the cockpit in a basin and if one generated too much suds by overuse of washing liquid there would be remonstration because that meant rinsing out the ware with more precious fresh water. Gearoid suggested once that we not stack the plates after the meal as that would obviate the need for washing the undersides of the plates. A lot of quirky stuff like that goes on in boats. Len once got annoyed at the sudden burst of industry cleaning up after the repast and remarked to me: 'One does not get a chance to enjoy that delightful lethargy that befalls one after an enjoyable meal.'

Len and I used to discuss the terminology of boating and how many of the terms have made their way into common (land) usage: he would say 'choc-a-block' and I'd respond, 'can't move'; 'swing a cat', 'no room'; 'swinging the lead', 'lazy so and so'. Another association we pondered was the way boat parts were named after things of the church: a tabernacle housed the ship's mast and a pulpit is the guard rail around the ship's prow. These were some of the things that occupied our discussions as well as rope work, signal flags and Morse code. Each trip introduced something new in the way of seamanship and personnel; everyone had something to offer, depending on their own individual skills.

Gearoid introduced me to cheese and marmalade on brown bread. Generally we provisioned well prior to setting off but we never had eggs on board – Gearoid would not allow them and I never found out the reason why. When we were shopping once before a voyage I slipped a dozen eggs into the shopping trolley to see if we'd get past the checkout with them. Len saw this move and remarked, 'O'Connor, you are playing with fire'. Sure enough, Gearoid spotted them at the checkout and the game was up. Len and I discussed the 'no eggs' rule occasionally and came up with different scenarios as to their banishment from the good ship we sailed in. One that I put forth was that in the past some crewman dropped eggs on the cabin sole and the gooey liquid subsequently made its way down into the bilges – the lowest part beneath the floor – and eventually began to stink to high heaven; rotting eggs emit one of the most objectionable odours known and the smell would linger a long time. Len had his own ideas on the ban and regretted that Eggs Florentine were off the menu on *An tSiochâin*. Me, I liked a boiled egg for breakfast from time to time and in later years on my own boat I made sure that eggs were always on board; there was a certain rebelliousness in this, I suppose, and whenever I'm having eggs at sea I naturally think of Gearoid and my days on *An tSiochâin*.

Chapter 4

GOD OF THE NORTH WIND

I have great memories from those days and it is not easy to pick an event, a time or place that stands out above the rest. In late June 1990 we sailed into Killary fjord between Galway and Mayo and anchored off Leenane, which would later be famous for the making of the film 'The Field'. The glacial fjord is one of three of its kind in Ireland and I was fascinated by its architecture over its ten-mile length. As we made our way along the fjord, the steep mountains on the northern side would occasionally reveal a gap through which a draught of air would rush and fill our sails as if Boreas himself, god of the north wind, was providing propulsion to move us along. In later years when I returned to Killary on *Eibhlís*, a friend on board remarked when this happened: 'Who left that window open?'

Sailing into Killary Harbour

That June voyage was also when I first met crewman Seamus O'Donoghue, a nephew of Gearoid's; our paths would cross several times in the future in various ports including St Mary's in the Isles of Scilly, Union Hall and Schull in West Cork, and Dingle, my home port. But that late June of 1990 was famous because it was when Ireland exited Italia '90 after being beaten by Italy on 30 June. The crew of *An tSiochâin* watched the game in what is now known as The Field pub in Leenane. That pleasant sojourn in Leenane (apart from Salvatore Schillaci's goal) was typical of the enjoyable aspects of voyaging in good company; one of those times which make up for the challenging and often worrying stints at sea. As is often said: 'It is not all plain sailing.'

After leaving Killary behind that year, the place stayed in my mind for a while; there was something about the place that I couldn't pin down. The words made famous by MacArthur came to mind: 'I came through and I shall return.'

***

Like all clubs and institutions, we who sail have a fraternity and in many ways we take our membership of this fraternity to be a serious and committed thing. We help the other today because tomorrow it might be you who needs assistance. There is an unwritten rule that states: those who go down to the sea in ships look out for each other. Several times over the years I have been offered crew when I was short-handed; a safe mooring in a harbour, or provisions when my boat was running low. In a later section, on *Eibhlís*, I will be recalling when I met two of Gearoid's nephews in the Isles of Scilly and how when they were in the midst of a serious adventure of their own they offered me kind assistance when I was sailing alone.

The Pierces and the O'Donoghues, nephews and nieces of Fr Gearoid, sailed frequently on *An tSiochâin*. Back then they were young, teenagers mostly, and it was evident that uncle Gearoid was held in high esteem by one and all. In his dealings with young people on board, Gearoid was firm and fair. If he gave a tongue-lashing over something done wrong – a mislaid winch handle, a line trailing over the side – he would later soothe the offender with kind words while also pointing out the possible outcomes of the infraction.

I believe that Gearoid had one particular fault, that being that he presumed that all who stepped on board the boat had prior knowledge of sailing. I remember several greenhorns in an agitated tizzy when instructed by our skipper to: 'haul in the main sheet'; 'cleat that halyard'; 'open the lazarette', etc. 'What ... what thing? Where?' would be their plea as they looked about frantically to see if any of the items mentioned bore any resemblance to things they had learned about at school. In time everyone knew what a halyard was, what it did and where it was cleated. Let me state here that there were no lashes (to the skin) given out on *An tSiochâin*. With Gearoid, our skipper and guardian while on his boat, it was important that he emphasised correct and orderly procedures. I have found, as a skipper myself, the necessity for such adherence to correct ways of doing things. With a view to the safety of the boat and its crew, a skipper must be able to see beyond the minor, seemingly inconsequential infraction to its possible outcome under different conditions. Although my approach may be different from Gearoid's when it comes to the instruction of newcomers, the fundamentals of orderliness and correct practice that I espouse are the same.

For instance, on my own boat once, a crewman had hauled up the mainsail, winched it tight and then cleated – so far so good – then he observed the local dolphin 'Fungie' putting on a show for the tourist boats and was enthralled for several minutes. Later I went on the foredeck and saw the winch handle teetering on the edge of the coach roof and the halyard in disarray on the deck. I had to let that deckhand know that one cannot get distracted or be forgetful while performing a task that can be vital to the ship's safe passage. We will get away with stuff on land often but at sea second chances are rare. Losing a winch handle may not be a big deal but having lines strewn about the deck, especially if the weather turns bad, can lead to several mishaps.

Chapter 5

Raz de Sein and Waiting out Weather in St Mary's

The Isles of Scilly, off Land's End, are a popular stopover for yachts cruising from Ireland to Cornwall and the North of France. The largest island in the group is St Mary's and *An tSiocháin* normally docked there when in the vicinity. St Mary's is scenic and relaxed and a pleasant place to spend a day or two before undertaking a long sailing leg. In Hugh Town there is a small Catholic church, Our Lady Star of the Sea, where visiting priests were welcome to say mass. In 1987, on a cruise to France, the crew of *An tSiocháin* had the church to themselves for a mass celebrated by Fr Gearoid. The rest of the crew that year was the aforementioned Len Breewood; James Drennan, a sail maker; and Riobárd Pierce, nephew of Gearoid. The intimacy of the small church and the small group of attendees made the event extra special. The garden at the rear of the church was in full bloom and we had a photo shoot on the grounds following the mass. A plaque was mounted on the rear wall to commemorate two ships, the *Ark* and the *Dove*, which, when en route to set up the colony of Maryland in the US in 1633, were separated in a storm off the south-west coast of England but were reunited months later in Barbados. On subsequent trips to the area it was a given that Gearoid would say mass in that small church and give thanks for a successful trip thus far and pray for a safe passage on the coming leg of the voyage.

Plaque in garden of St. Mary's church, Isles of Scilly

That year, after St Mary's, we sailed on south to Brittany and on the way passed the Raz de Sein, a stretch of water west of Pointe du Raz in north-west France. To the west lies the island of Île de Sein and beyond that a crop of rocks and smaller islands that I'm sure would frighten the life out of you in a gale. A passage south from England and Ireland passes through this patch of water between the Pointe and the Île de Sein. It was here that I first learned about the necessity of knowing the tides; there is a six-knot race (thus 'Raz') of water at spring tides at this stretch. This effectively means that if a yacht would normally make six knots at this position, the yacht would be stationary if going against the current at high springs. Conversely, if the boat is going with the current, a very fast ride is guaranteed when passing through the Raz. Forward planning is very important when a passage has conditions like this in its path.

Ile de Sein, North Brittany

We sailed south as far as Pornic after stopping in Morgat, Concarneau and Lorient on the way. We spent days enjoying great weather, wonderful cuisine and a smattering of open-air jazz and various Celtic entertainments in the towns we visited. After a pleasant sojourn in Pornic, we pointed *An tSiochháin* back northward for the homeward leg. We anchored off Belle Île eight hours later and went for a walk on the island. At 0150 the following morning there was an early call – 'all hands on deck' – as our anchor had started dragging and we were gaining on a rocky shore. Len, who appeared on deck in the nip, as he was accustomed to sleeping that way, was advised to return to the cabin and suit up lest a further calamity be brought upon us by his nakedness. We all scrambled and helped to make the boat ready to sail out to sea and set a course for Bénodet, where we stayed for a day before moving on to Audierne which was our last stop on the French coast before making for the south of Ireland.

On the way home we encountered strong northerly winds south of the Isles of Scilly and opted for a layover on the islands until conditions became more favorable. These islands were to figure largely in my sailing life for a good number of years; during the eighties with Gearoid and subsequently under my own steam, as it were. While the islands are scenic and charming, if one is committed to their confines waiting out a storm it is another matter. A sailor may be grateful for the islands' hospitality after making off harbour following a rough time at sea but the islands can become mildly oppressive after five or six days. It may be more agreeable for people who are used to island life to linger in such places, but for a mainlander like me, wider options are favoured.

We were to be bound to the islands for an indeterminate number of days and Len, Riobárd and James felt that their commitments at home demanded their return. This is understandable. When going on a sailing trip the exigencies of date and time cannot always be adhered to. To put it simply, they jumped ship and travelled home overland while Gearoid and I stayed with the boat to wait out the storm. This was to be my first time taking up a prolonged residence in the vicinity of the islands.

My skipper and I passed the time exploring the coastline by land; having lunch ashore in Hugh Town; visiting the church where Gearoid would say mass; doing odd jobs around the boat; and the big event of every day: listening to the weather forecast on BBC radio, which we would do three times a day.

Then we would spend time doing a deeper exploration of the island; find more jobs to do on the boat, etc., etc. I would go off on my own from time to time and visit the local taverns. That, too, got monotonous after a time. All the while we were anchored in the north harbour of St Mary's and using the dinghy to go ashore. The smallest task was given an importance beyond its true value; going ashore to buy postcards and spending an hour writing was a huge adventure which distracted us from the 'wait'. What were we waiting for? The wind had been very strong from the north since we made landfall – that was the worst possible condition for us. We were thirty hours from the south of Ireland – and that would be in fair weather. We were waiting for a south-westerly preferably or indeed any wind that didn't have north as a prefix in its name.

After the fourth day the weather started to abate and on the fifth, after discussing the possible sea state following a prolonged blow and the fact that at best we would be out here for a day and a quarter, we set sail. *An tSiochâin* was manageable with a reduced crew once there were no serious weather issues to contend with. We had a good trip home; we shared the watches, told stories and sang songs. During the night, we had a clear sky, which rendered the compass redundant as the North Star gave us guidance to the south of Ireland.

About twenty miles out from West Cork, the wind had freshened a good bit and the sea had built itself into hills and troughs to the extent that a fishing boat about a mile away got lost intermittently between the waves. I watched as the fishing boat, which was accompanied by a flock of excited gulls, ducked out of sight briefly and rose again through a breaking wave. I was at the wheel, thinking how welcome the sight of another vessel can be when you think you are alone with the vastness of the sea. Gearoid was nonchalantly perched on top of the cockpit coaming, looking like he was at complete ease with what was going on around him. He had a knack of appearing casual and unconcerned by situations where other crew might be harbouring doubts. As we got near the coast, the sight of land was blocked from us for a long time by the high seas. Eventually a white blur, representing Galley Head lighthouse, appeared in the distance off to starboard. About an hour later we were in Glandore Bay and soon after we had the Island of Adam to port. This island would achieve notoriety in January 2012 when five fishermen lost their lives in the tragedy of the *Tit Bonhomme.* After leaving Adam behind we soon had the smaller island of Eve to port in the inner harbor. There is a local maxim that advises sailors to 'avoid Adam and to hug Eve.'

It was my first time sailing in to Union Hall and in the years that followed it would become my most-visited harbour. As one gets into the inner end of the channel, two harbours reveal themselves: Union Hall, which is home to a sizeable fishing fleet, on the left, and Glandore, which has a sailing club and various leisure craft using its anchorages, on the right. In strong south-easterly winds Glandore is open to the onslaught of the sea while Union Hall gives more shelter as it is tucked round the corner to the west.

On the way up the channel, *An tSiocháin*'s keel scraped on outlying rock that extended underwater from the perch which marked it as a danger – a thing of little consequence, the scraping, but mischievously I thought silently about Gearoid's fallibility. We docked at the old pier in Union Hall and my skipper thanked me for my company and assistance in bringing the boat home as we stretched our legs on the pier. We walked to the village for rations and I called to Moloney's pub to say hello to two of my former shipwright students, Johnny and Finbar Moloney, who came from that house. In subsequent years, that house/pub would become a land base of mine whenever I visited the area. Gearoid and I set sail in the evening again, bound for *An tSiocháin's* home port, Fenit in north Kerry. The weather had moderated and we looked forward to a pleasant evening sail along the southern coast and then overnight up along the western seaboard and home.

Much later, after a sleep while Gearoid was on watch, I awoke in my bunk to see the sweep of the lantern from Bull Rock lighthouse. The darkness was intermittently broken by the shafts of light. A south-westerly breeze nudged us on our way northwards and the only sound was the swish of broken water as the boat cut through the surface. The boat had full main and foresails decently pulling the vessel towards home. Gearoid was at the wheel when I looked through the open cabin hatch. The light would briefly reveal his face and move on to return fifteen seconds later. There was a certain magic at play which I had not witnessed before. The darkness and stillness of the night – it was actually around 0300 hours – being momentarily interrupted by the beam from somewhere far off in the distance enthralled me. It was like being in a separate world without another living creature or distraction. I stayed inside the hatch for a while counting the seconds between the flashes. In between I would look through the cabin porthole towards the origin of this Super Trouper light of thousands of candlepower and think of the Abba song:

Bull Rock lighthouse at night

Tonight the super trouper lights are gonna find me …

On the way south on this voyage with our full crew, we had seen the hole nature had bored through the Bull Rock, which was home to this magnificent light. Then we had gone inside Dursey Island, through the sound on a southbound stream with a fair wind while above our heads the cable car travelled from island to mainland – that was another first for me.

I announced myself to Gearoid and relieved him at the helm; he advised me of the compass course and that the next thing to look out for on the way north was the Lemon Rock, which was east of the Skelligs and west of Puffin Island. Gearoid went down to take a nap, leaving me alone, full of trepidation over the Lemon Rock and its exact geographical position. My most earnest desire at that time was that 'never the twain shall meet' – my position and that of the rock. This was before GPS chart plotters but my skipper had assured me that if I maintained the bearing we would be well clear and, besides, the event was hours away. The event, I thought, what does he mean by that? Still, I was uneasy, my navigation skills were still wanting refinement at that stage and it would take a few more years before I got to know and trust the GPS. I couldn't help wondering 'what if?'

Time pushed the light beam from the Bull behind me. Its intensity was diminishing by the minute and I wished it had thousands more candlepower to light up the sea to the north and show me this confounded Lemon Rock. After a time the light from Skellig Michael beckoned from the north-west. At least that would keep me company until dawn broke. Gearoid had not been below for long; he needed rest and I didn't want to bother him with my concerns. I looked at the chart and the pencil line of our track and the position of the rock and thought, 'Who am I to second guess Gearoid O'Donnchadha, GOD?', and knuckled down to my watch. At about the time we were due to be in the vicinity of the Lemon, the dawn was coming. The Skelligs soon revealed their peaks and later, further to the east (of the Skelligs), the hump of the Lemon appeared – and, as if he had it timed, Gearoid also appeared from the cabin. He had told me once that whenever he was off watch and in his bunk, he could never switch off fully; he stayed attuned to the sounds of the boat and the course it was on and could tell from the sound of the sails if there was a shift in the wind. The next landmark was always on his mind, whether it was a rock, a headland or a due landfall. In later years I knew exactly what he was talking about; I always choose the bunk nearest the companionway so I am always at the ready.

I took a break after the Lemon and Gearoid called me a couple of hours later to come up and see a spectacle. I came up and beheld one of the most spectacular sights I had ever witnessed. We were two thirds of the way across Dingle bay and ahead the Blasket Islands were majestic as they reached skywards in all their jagged splendour from the flat table of water on which they seemed to float. I did a full three-sixty-degree turn to my right, taking in Slea Head and the Eagle and Brandon mountains; then up the bay to Dingle and beyond and round by the Iveragh Peninsula to Bray Head; then out to the Skelligs and the wide expanse of sea to the west. The panoramic snapshot from that position was one of splendour. The sun had broken free from the sea and coloured the half-dome above us in countless hues from gold to blue. In later years I would see a seascape to beat this – that would be sea and sky – but for a combination of land, sea and sky, that one on that July day will take beating. After tying up at Fenit, I calculated that we had voyaged over nine hundred nautical miles over the course of the return journey.

Chapter 6
The Wolf

The coast of Cornwall has a ruggedness and beauty which has been formed over millennia by storm-lashed seas. The daring toe of Land's End sticks out into the Atlantic as if challenging the elements to do their worst. The coastline is strewn with wrecks to such an extent that wall posters marking the positions of the unfortunate doomed vessels are available to tourists in the local shops. Lighthouses now abound in the area in an effort to ward off the modern sailor from the most lethal of its rocks. It is along this coast that I first became aware of the majesty and nobility of these lighthouses.

On another trip to Cornwall, Gearoid and I were on deck as the weather turned nasty. 'Where is the wolf?' Gearoid shouted above the wind. We were sailing from St Mary's with the aim of making off Penzance. A strong south-easterly wind was blowing and about an hour after we set out, very squally conditions developed. It was a clear run to the Runnel Stone cardinal mark, south of Land's End, except for the Wolf Rock which lay in our path, though south of our track, three quarters of the distance eastwards. We were beating towards Land's End, meaning we were close-hauled and sailing as close to the wind as possible. The term 'beating' describes us as the ones 'slapping' the sea as we progressed; it could also be interpreted as the sea giving us a battering. When close-hauled under such circumstances, further progress towards the wind is not possible; the best generally that modern sailing boats can make towards the wind, on a given tack, is about forty-five degrees. The situation for us as we headed towards the Runnel Stone was that the track we were on and the direction of the wind made that precise angle. When leeway was factored in (that is, the slippage of the boat away from the wind), it meant that we were being pushed off our tack and gaining to the north – there was just a little too much of an easterly push in the south-easterly wind. About halfway across we decided to tack to the south for a time to better position us for making off the eastern side of the toe of Land's End.

With the freshening wind we were well heeled over and intermittently we were being pelted with heavy rain from the squalls. For forty-five minutes we stayed on that tack and went about during an opening in the grey sky. We saw the Wolf and its lighthouse in the distance and it looked like we would be south of it as we made for the east. A couple of minutes later the sky closed in again and the squalls intensified. The Wolf was the elephant in the room as we beat eastwards. The sky would open again and I would get a fuzzy glimpse of the rock in the distance. 'There,' I would point to Gearoid as I readied at the winches for a call to go about again. For a lot of the time we were blind to the body of water and the solitary obstruction in our path. The fog horn from the Wolf would sound and I thought it was the most lonesome sound in the world. A shaft of light would occasionally burst through the clouds above our heads and linger awhile before the clouds closed in again, leaving us blind once more. We held our tack while Gearoid estimated our proximity to the guardian of the rock. Our hope was that we would pass it on the southern side. And so we did. As we neared, the sky cleared and we found we were safely to the south of the rock, but we were not out of the woods yet.

The Wolf Rock seen through a squall

While we gained on Land's End, the ferocity of the squalls intensified and again we were being pushed north. It was turning into a slog against the elements in the hairiest section of coastline in Western Europe. Looking back, it was probably the only time on *An tSiochháin* that I felt unease. It takes time to get to know a sailing yacht: what she can take;

at which angle of heel she performs best; how much sail can she carry in heavy weather, etc. This was one of my earlier voyages and my knowledge of yacht behaviour was limited and I was only in the process of getting to know the boat. At that time by the Wolf I forgot that the deck on which I stood had spent thirty days in the Atlantic in God knows what weather. It takes a wide range of weather conditions at sea and varying sea states to realise the true capabilities of any boat. When you get over a trying ordeal brought about by the weather, you find that you have moved along on the learning curve. Then the next time you learn a bit more.

Between the Wolf and the mainland, Gearoid made a decision to head north and I eased off the sheets and we made for St Ives on the north-western corner of Land's End. The reasoning for this decision was sound and I would understand its true significance much later: had we eventually rounded Land's End and started heading east along the Cornish coast we would for a time have a lee shore to worry about and in freshening weather that is a sailor's worst nightmare. It was easier to go northward as the wind and sea were in our favour. We soon left the Wolf behind and over two hours later we sailed into St Ives and tied up at the quay wall.

St Ives. Don't you just love those Cornish place names? Truro, Penzance, St Just ... They were all familiar to me from novels I had read that were set in Cornwall. St Ives is a picturesque seaside town which at one time was a commercial fishing port. The quay dries out at low tide so we were crunched into soft sand at the wall in the morning. We took a walk on the beach right up to *An tSiochháin* just for a look at the good old girl who had once again brought us safely in. We left on the next tide and rounded Land's End, giving a nod to the Wolf looking imposing away to the west in the clear day. Then we made for Penzance, and that corner of Cornwall is one I would visit often in the future.

There are many beautiful spots that unfortunately do not lend themselves to yachting because of their inaccessibility, their exposure to prevailing winds, or the tidal pattern which dries them out. St Ives is one of these places. I have not been back to St Ives. I often say when I arrive at a Cornish port by boat that I must go back to St Ives by road. I haven't done it yet. When I see it on the chart or hear its name I always associate it with the time the Wolf was at our door and I was getting to know *An tSiochháin* in the early eighties.

Chapter 7

THE FRIENDLY DOLPHIN AND *An tSiochâin*'s SCARY INCIDENT

In the summer of 1982, *An tSiochâin* was at anchor in La Baie des Trepasses, north of Pointe du Raz in Brittany, awaiting the turn of the tide to round the headland with the stream. The bay was a curved inlet with a beach that glistened with white sand. Another yacht, flying the German ensign, was anchored a hundred metres away. Soon after settling to anchor, a young bottlenose dolphin appeared and gave *An tSiochâin* a thorough inspection. During the dolphin's playful antics in the vicinity of the anchor chain he was christened Pierre by the crew. The logbook for the day does not explain how the name came about. I suspect that Len Breewood, who was on that cruise, came up with it. Pierre would occasionally wander over towards the German boat for a look but it was decided by the crew of *An tSiochâin* that Pierre's forays in that direction were perfunctory and that his undoubted preference was for playing beside *An tSiochâin*.

Gearoid jumped in the water and made to swim down along the length of the anchor chain, about 15 metres, to the seabed. Pierre, who had been nosing the anchor, gave Gearoid a fright as he suddenly left the anchor and came up at speed along the chain but just before they collided Pierre bore away and followed him along the chain and back up to break the surface together. Pierre stayed playing around the boat and later when it was time to weigh anchor and head for the Raz, he seemed to follow the boat out of the small bay and then took the lead as if guiding the boat to its next destination, Audierne, around the corner from the Pointe du Raz. It was clear Pierre had taken a shine to *An tSiochâin* and its crew, who regularly applauded and encouraged his display.

The next day *An tSiochâin* continued south along the Brittany coast and five days later returned again to Audierne to overnight before returning home the following day. At 0530 the next morning, 26 July, just after dawn, *An tSiochâin* left Audierne, rounded the Raz, the vicinity in which Pierre had fallen in love with the boat, and plotted a course for the south of Ireland. In the dark of morning, unbeknownst to the sleepy-eyed crew, it was possible that Pierre was again guiding *An tSiochâin* onward as she headed for home. On this return trip from Brittany to Fenit, *An tSiochâin* would not stop at any other port on the way. At 1210 on the twenty-eighth, Mizen Head was abeam and eight hours later *An tSiochâin* was crossing Dingle bay as she made for the Blasket Sound and the final leg. On the trip northwards, none of the crew thought to look in their wake to see if Pierre was following.

An tSiochâin's return to Dingle Bay in 1982 – with company?

The following year it was noticed that a young bottlenose dolphin was appearing regularly in Dingle Bay. The dolphin eventually settled in a patch close to the entrance to Dingle Harbour. Some say the dolphin was there as early as the autumn of 1982. That dolphin has since been named Fungie and has become a major tourist attraction for Dingle. As I write, thirty years later, Fungie is still playfully welcoming the boats that enter the harbour.

A couple of years after *An tSiochâin's* return from Audierne, I was on board as she cruised round to Dingle from Fenit. It was the Sunday of the Dingle regatta. As *An tSiochâin* approached the harbour, Fungie appeared alongside us and gave an excited display at the prow of the boat, just as Pierre had done in the bay north of Pte du Raz. He stayed with us for a long time and eventually led the way into Dingle harbour. Was this Pierre? Had he followed *An tSiochâin* that dark morning in 1982 to usher her safely home? Who knows?

***

On the following cruise, 1983, we had Angela Kelly, a colleague from the college onboard. Our destination was Penzance by way of the Isles of Scilly. After we had settled in at the small inner harbour in Penzance, where the water level is controlled by a gate which is open for about three hours on either side of high water, Angela and I hired bicycles and spent a number of hours touring around Land's End. The day was very warm and a gentle wind helped keep the heat at bay on our route which took in a number of small but very quaint hamlets like Sennan Cove and St. Just. On our round of the coast there were fantastic views out to sea of the North Atlantic Ocean.

Before leaving Penzance, our crew went on a two and a half mile walk along the beach to the east of Penzance; this brought us to St. Michael's Mount, a small tidal island in Mounts Bay. The island is linked to the town of Marazion by a paved walkway about a third of a mile long. The walkway is passable only from mid to low tide. The island is home to the chapel of St. Michael whose tower once acted as a landmark for sailors making off the island. The castle atop the granite rock is 250 feet above sea level. Low-lying houses are situated facing the mainland on the northern side and are separated from the castle above by dense greenery, thus the Cornish translation for the name for the island: 'the grey rock in a wood'. Mount Saint-Michel in Normandy was considered historically to be a counterpart to the Cornish Mount; both share similar physical characteristics and tidal conditions. The island was also said to be the home of a giant named Cormoran who walked to the mainland at night to steal sheep and other animals to supplement his diet.

At full tide the rock and its castle, viewed from landward, look stunning emerging from the sea. When visiting the island as a pedestrian, one must keep an eye on the tide to avoid being stranded, though I can think of worse places to be cut off from the world at large. Later that year I saw the island from the air in a James Bond film, *Never Say Never*, as cruise missiles shot over it as they left the Cornish coast on the way out to sea.

Angela left the cruise after a couple of days in Penzance and travelled overland to fulfil other arrangements. *An tSiocháin* continued cruising in the Cornwall vicinity going eastwards as far as Falmouth before making for The Isles of Scilly on the homeward leg.

Three hours after leaving Falmouth *An tSiocháin* was off Lizard Point at 2020 hours and steering a magnetic course of 274° for Peninnis Head lighthouse, the southernmost point of the island of St Mary's in the Scilly Isles, where we intended to break the journey home. Three hours later we were abeam the Wolf Rock and south by three miles. We expected to pick up the light from Peninnis lighthouse through the darkness of the night, which had turned foul. As the throw, or range, of the Peninnis light was twenty miles, it should have been visible momentarily. Donal O'Donoghue (Fr Gearoid's nephew) was at the helm. A strong southerly wind was blowing and the air was filled with water. The prow of the boat was barely visible from the cockpit.

From the Wolf it was nineteen miles to Peninnis Head, which when rounded opened up the sound leading to the northern and southern harbours of Hugh Town. Under sail with the Wolf behind us, we were gaining to the west, doing about five knots. *An tSiocháin* didn't have GPS fitted back then. The trailing log would be checked hourly for speed over the water and the reading transferred to the logbook. In the situation we were in it was crucial that the helmsman maintained the given compass course. The Isles of Scilly and all of their outlying rocks were dead ahead.

While *An tSiocháin* was estimated to be within range of the Peninnis light, the bad visibility must have obscured the beam as the sky revealed nothing but black all round, broken occasionally by lightning flashes. As our estimated landfall at the headland approached, the odd bolt of lightning would crack the sky open and add to the miseries of the night and as time passed an understandable sense of unease developed. At 0230 hours I was down below when I heard the roar of the engine shatter the silence of the cabin. I rushed to the cockpit and heard Gearoid shouting, 'Down sails, down sails', while he turned the boat to port through an angle of 180° to get back on the reciprocal course of 094°. I helped with furling the sails and wondered what calamity had struck us. We were going on a course almost due east – back the way we came.

When we had regained composure Gearoid told me what happened. And much had happened! It seems that calamity does not come singly. Gearoid had taken shelter below for a couple of hours when something urged him back to the cockpit. He felt later that it may have been anxiety about having given the exact course for Peninnis Head rather than something closer to 265°, some ten degrees to the south, which would open up the light in good time. Anxiety to shorten the journey through the small hours of a brutal night can affect one's judgement! No sooner had he arrived in the cockpit than a bolt of lightning struck the yacht. There came a sizzling crack like a firework exploding and all the lights, navigational and instrument lights alike, went out. After some seconds they came back on. Now another anxiety struck home. The lightning had struck the lightning conductor at the top of the mast; this conductor was earthed to a bronze plate on the outside of the hull below the water line. The worry was that lightning has been known to blow this plate off the hull, sometimes leaving a gaping hole with predictable consequences. *An tSiocháin* mercifully escaped this fate and survived the incident unharmed. Relief did not last long. Another bolt of lightning lit up the sea around the boat and Gearoid and Donal found themselves looking down on a large rock fifty metres to starboard. Almost instantaneously another bolt of lightning hit rocks less than 100 metres to port. Gearoid immediately took the helm and turned full lock to port while starting the engine. He had decided to retreat, like a bat out of hell. All that we could determine at the time of the event was that we had to be somewhere in the vicinity of the Scilly Isles, but the darkness of the morning called for prudence and the reciprocal course ensured, we hoped, a safe track. As Gearoid put it, 'If I get in through a gap, I hope to get out the same gap!' Modern GPS instruments memorise and plot the boat's track on a screen and make sailing back on this same track easy, but pre-GPS it was crucial to keep a log of your bearing and any course changes implemented. It is recommended that one always knows the reciprocal bearing as it is no mean feat to add or subtract 180° to or from the given course, especially when under pressure.

After a time going east and then south, where there was clear water, we waited for dawn and eventually got our bearings. We accepted that the visibility was so bad that Peninnis light had not been visible when we needed it. We sailed into Hugh Town at 0640 hours. Gearoid subsequently identified on the chart where we were at half past two in the morning when the light from above broke through the gloom of the dark and lit up the rocks. We had made leeway of about 2.5 miles to the north and were entering a gap between a group of about twenty rocks and small islands to the south-east of the island of St Martin. The leeway that had accrued since the Wolf Rock – over a distance of nineteen miles –is understandable in hindsight. Under normal circumstances it is quite difficult for even the most experienced helmsman to maintain a compass course. In this case the helmsman seems to have done very well given the atrocious conditions prevailing. Another explanation for the deviation might be a magnetic anomaly in the area. These anomalies are localised in various areas and are due to a departure from the normal magnetic field of the earth because of concentrated deposits of iron in the substratum. Such anomalies have been identified in the Scilly Isles area. The consequence of the anomaly is a 'throw-off' of the compass bearing, which results in an erroneous course being followed.

Gearoid told me when I was researching the logbook for this work that the incident described here was the scariest he had experienced in all his years at sea; he believes that the bolt of lightning struck just in time to get *An tSiochháin* out of danger. Based on the circumstances of the incident and the undoubted influence that our skipper has on high, it may be reasonable to conclude that our safe passage out of danger was due to divine intervention.

Chapter 8

A Hard Act to Follow

For most of the summers in the eighties I sailed with Gearoid on *An tSiocháin* and by the end of the decade I had amassed a bank of knowledge about sailing, seamanship and navigation, which prepared me for the natural progression to ownership of my own vessel. The years with Gearoid built my confidence and made me look at the sea anew. Though I was born on the shores of the harbour and had served an apprenticeship in boatbuilding at the local yard, I had not, in my young years, fallen for the sea. Apart from forays into rowing in the harbour and the trips in the bay on newly launched trawlers on sea trials, my *grá* for the sea was strangely perfunctory; there was no romance, no awe, no 'gee, I must do that again'. And when I left that life behind to pursue one of teaching and the classroom, I thought that was the end of me and boats. Then, as alluded to earlier, two things happened, three years apart, which steered me back to boats and the sea. I got a position teaching shipwright apprentices in a college in Tralee, and Gearoid and I became colleagues and friends when he joined the staff there. I am a sailor today because of the convergence of these events.

Apart from the skills I acquired under Gearoid's wing, there were other things that instilled a love of the sea in me to which I cannot do justice with the written word. To transcribe to paper the smell of seawater in the air on a calm evening in summer is as difficult as trying to describe the smell of newly mown grass to a desert dweller. The sound of a hull powered by a sail, cutting through the sea on an otherwise silent night is for the ear only; and the sound of a furious wind as it rushes past spars and rigging, trying to sweep away anything in its path that is not fixed down, is a music which both scares and gives pause to wonder at the natural might of the elements. The sting of saltwater on the cheeks from a whippet of sea tossed your way by the wind and the dry crust it leaves when the sun shines again joins a list of sensations which do not lend themselves to transcription. The package of elemental wonders, in light and darkness, that assails the sailor is of a uniqueness which is rare in any other form of endeavour. On a personal level, courage and weakness conflict, as do confidence and apprehension, on a very different scale at sea compared to on-land activities. The sea engenders humility. The sea instils an awareness of one's abilities and if a sailor, be he a skipper or deckhand, is not up to the mark, there is no place to hide in the confines of his vessel; not that it is a prerequisite to be gung-ho while taking on the sea, but it demands a diligence and honesty that cannot be faked.

An tSiocháin was my home for hundreds of hours while I traversed the seas over ten summers along the Atlantic seaboard of Ireland, Cornwall and Brittany. It was the vessel whose performance I would compare with future yachts of my own and any other I sailed in. She was a hard act to follow in many respects. On several points of sailing in challenging weather her behaviour was commendable. She was solid when bedded down in her course like a ploughshare in a furrow. Her accommodations were spacious and while down below in heavy weather one did not notice the turbulent sea beyond her twelve-millimetre skin of reinforced glass. The rod rigging that supported her mast reached skyward to a point fifty-two feet aloft at the head. I once hung on a halyard from its highest block on a bosun's chair and marvelled at the sleek lines of the gunwales below and the cheeky contour of the counter stern at deck level.

In 1991 I went on my last cruise on *An tSiocháin*. She would go on skippered by Gearoid and crew, one of whom would occupy my upper port-side bunk, on voyages to Norway, La Coruña in Spain and several ports in Brittany. She would navigate the Caledonia Canal, visit the Faeroes and the Hebrides and return often to Gearoid's favourite place: the island of Iona on Scotland's west coast. Gearoid now sails in a new vessel, *Aqua Viva*.

In 2002 *An tSiocháin* changed ownership and had a major refit. Her new owner, Patsy Fegan, told me he actually had to sit for an interview with Fr Gearoid, who wanted to know if he was suitable and had the necessary skill sets to take on the now famous ship and most of all that he would mind her and be good to her. Patsy duly took possession and was amazed at the boat's speed and overall sailing ability. In 2010 *An tSiocháin* came second in a race from Crosshaven to La Rochelle, the ten-yearly event named La Coupe des Trois Phares (The Three Lighthouses Cup). Patsy and his crew, made up of Crosshaven RNLI members, took the silver cup from a fleet of over eighty boats, which included French,

English and Belgian sailors. *An tSiocháin* proved a big hit with the other competitors and was complimented on her ability and gracefulness.

Following her twenty years of sailing up and down the Irish coast with Gearoid at the helm, *An tSiocháin,* which was a familiar sight each summer, became known as 'GOD's boat'. Patsy related a wonderful story to me regarding an incident during his first year of ownership. He was sailing *An tSiocháin* alone in West Cork and went down below to put on a pot of tea. While below, the sails slackened and started flapping in the wind. Over the VHF radio Patsy heard the voice: '... calling *An tSiocháin* ... calling *An tSiocháin*, your sails are flapping.' It was Fr Gearoid sailing by in his new boat *Aqua Viva*. Patsy muttered to himself, 'I see why they call him GOD. He *is* everywhere.'

As with all boats with which one has enjoyed a long association, one gets close to the ship and begins to regard the inanimate object as something endearing, especially when the boat has seen you through 'thick and thin'. I started yacht sailing on a top-of-the-range cruising boat. She was trustworthy and sure-footed and bore all of her charges to their destination without giving them cause for concern along the way. While my preference for a sailing yacht is that it is made of wood, that is a pronouncement I am reluctant to bandy about within earshot of *An tSiocháin*.

With that last statement I feel like I have betrayed her (*An tSiocháin*) and her gracious hospitality over a decade while she cradled me as I learned the ropes, but deep down I am a traditionalist when it comes to boats, having spent my apprenticeship years building wooden fishing trawlers. I believe that the craft involved in producing a vessel from wood is an exceptional form of endeavour and that the human input involved in forming the backbone, ribs and superstructure into a seaworthy boat is a labour guided by heart as well as hand. Not to mention the natural buoyancy properties of timber, the solidity of its mass as it pounds the sea, and the warm timber furnishings below where one lives through a voyage.

It is no wonder then to you readers that my own boats would be made from wood. In the following chapters you will meet them. And though I now bid *An tSiocháin* adieu, she and her crew will crop up from time to time in the following chapters. Her legacy is ever present in my sailing life and her majesty endures.

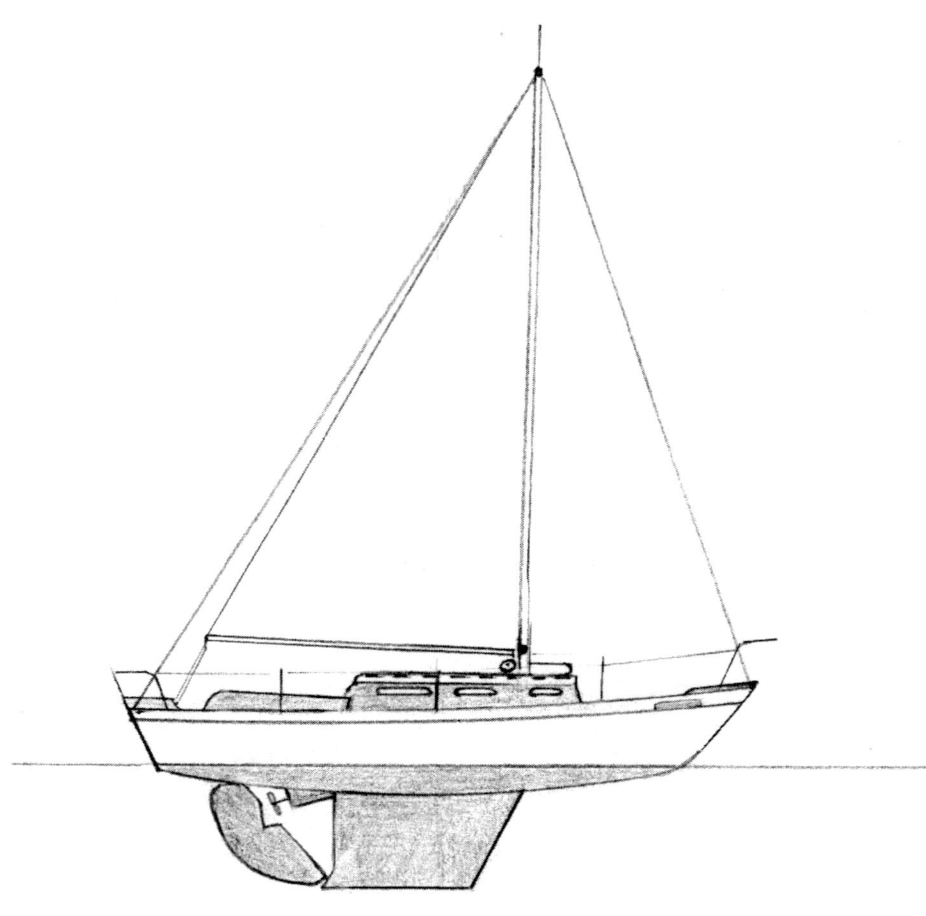

Part Two

Polyanna

(Windward and Whippet)

Chapter 1

LEN AND I GET A HUGE LIFT

During the period sailing with Fr Gearoid, I abandoned him one summer to crew with Len Breewood who had gotten a job delivering a boat from Dún Laoghaire to Lough Derg. On a warm mid-July day we set sail down the east coast on a thirty-foot fiberglass yacht named *Windward.* Len was putting a week aside for the trip and wanted to treat it as a leisurely cruise rather than a job tied to a strict timetable. It would be my first voyage with Len as skipper. That trip was nearly thirty years ago and I don't have the notes from the log that I kept on the way but I remember the highlights clearly.

I was still learning the ropes at that stage and was glad to be second in command, albeit in a crew of two, on a voyage which would cover more than three hundred and fifty nautical miles. We made a long run down the east coast and after turning the corner at Carnsore Point made off Dunmore East fishing harbour. Len cooked some excellent meals on the journey. One I can remember as being particularly succulent was spare ribs, which were marinated and oven cooked and served with baked potatoes and one of Len's special sauces.

After a couple of stopovers along the south coast, we pulled into Dingle Harbour and tied up next to a fishing boat for a night. I introduced Len to my parents and we took them for a spin on the bay before departing next day for the northern side of the Dingle Peninsula and on to the Shannon estuary. My father, Michael, who was a fisherman in his younger years, was showing Len the marks in the harbour, which in those days was not dredged or marked by channel buoys. I heard him impart a story to Len about a local harbour pilot who was guiding a boat into the harbour and was asked by the captain as they struck, 'How many sand banks are there in the harbour?', to which the pilot replied, 'Two, and when you get off this one, I will show you where the other one is.'

From Dingle Bay we went north through the Blasket Sound and made north-east for Kerry Head on an overnighter. Len was well versed in astro-navigation and pointed out several prominent stars and constellations along the way. Loop Head lighthouse was to our port side for most of the early morning, flashing its lantern four times every twenty seconds. We discussed the characteristics of lighthouses and the importance of their individual beams and flashes to mariners. In the centuries before the GPS age, they stood tall and were essential in providing safe passage during the darkened hours. They were, and still are, held in awe by the sailor. The solidity of their imposing structure, built to withstand ferocious weather in isolated places, is astonishing. Len and I talked about the lighthouses that have it easy, as it were, compared with the ones out at sea, at the mercy of the elements many miles from shore. Later that day, we passed Scattery Island in the Shannon Estuary and reckoned that the lighthouse on the island was definitely in contention for the one with the cushiest number in Ireland.

In the bright of morning we were at the mouth of the Shannon with Kilrush around twelve miles ahead. The leg from Kilrush to Limerick city was particularly interesting for me as it involved navigating in the river, where maintaining strict adherence to the port and starboard markers was vital. The experience was also a good learning experience because seven years later I would be doing a similar delivery on my own. When we arrived at the docks in Limerick, there was a crane on standby to take down our mast, which would be laid along the top of our deck and tied down. Nearly a dozen low bridges would be encountered before we got to Killaloe, where the mast would be hoisted again.

The next stage of the journey demanded keen attention to the navigation charts and the relevant data regarding the clearance of the bridges, the specs of our boat and the state of the tide when the bridges were approached. *Windward* had a draught of four and a half feet and a freeboard of three feet, added to which there was about another two and a half feet of cabin top and the stowed mast. What all that means is that we needed at least four and a half feet of water to float and at least five and a half feet clearance between the water level and the top of the bridge arch – truly an exercise in mathematics when the rise and fall of the tide had to be factored in. If the water level was too high, we wouldn't fit under the bridge and if it was too low, we would strike ground.

Len's knowledge and experience was invaluable and the whole exercise was a boon to me in my early days of navigating. The progress along the river was deliberately slow as we meandered with the water towards our most interesting barrier, Ardnacrusha, where a new experience awaited us.

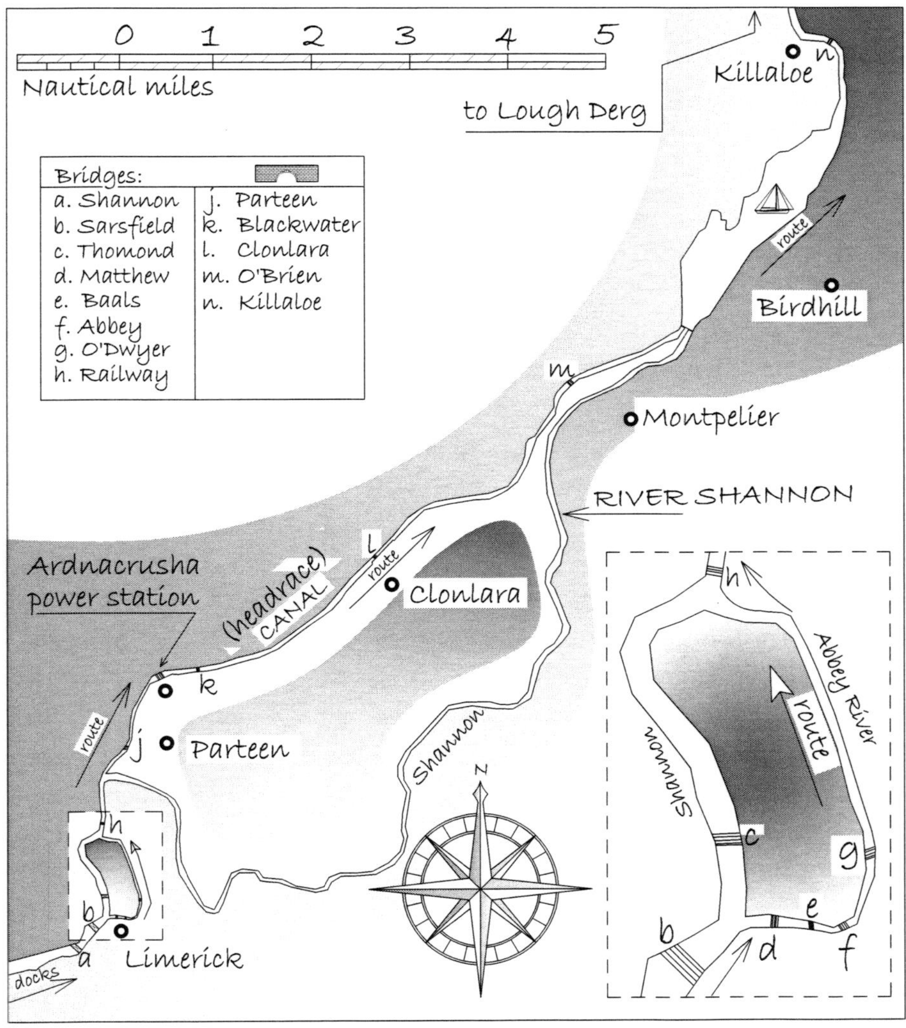

The sailing directions 1838–9 state:

The water communications between these two towns (Limerick and Killaloe) is carried on, partly by means of the river, and partly by three connecting canals on which there are eleven locks; but the whole of the navigation is in a very neglected state.

That was then. In mid to late 1920s, the Ardnacrusha power station was built; the water from the Shannon (and Lough Derg) was diverted below Killaloe via canal and dammed at Ardnacrusha, where a double lock was built and four turbines installed.

When the dam was constructed, there was a build-up of 100 feet of water above the level (of water) on the downstream side. In other words, the difference in the water level between Killaloe and Limerick was about 100 feet. The double lock has two chambers, with the lower chamber having a 40-foot lift (this 40 feet is 'about forty' because the Shannon is tidal as far as Ardnacrusha, resulting in a fluctuating water level) and the upper chamber having a 60-foot lift. A consequence of the dam is that, like with all dams, when the water is discharged through the turbines, it creates a wash which gathers pace as it flows downriver. Sailors navigating the river have to be aware of this. If the four turbines are discharged together, a four-knot stream will build up. If an ebbing spring tide and a water discharge from the dam along with a flood from rain occurs at the same time, a significant rate of knots will build up going downriver. A peak flow of more than ten knots was once recorded under Matthew Bridge in Limerick. Waiting stages are provided on each side of the dam where boats can tie up until the locks open – these times are noted in the sailing directions for the river.

With the tides and the heights of bridges to consider, along with the millions of gallons of water coming at a boat from the dam, you might think that any sailor would be out of his mind to tackle such a journey – believe me, it is much more fun than going by road. Len, who had his sums done, and I cleared all our bridges without incident, though we had to wait a bit here and there for the right combination of water beneath and free air over our heads.

We had a short wait for the lock to open. Another vessel was waiting with us. A huge gate opened upwards and we moved in to the long, narrow, box-like cavern which was about 110-feet long by 20-feet wide. The gate slid down behind us and the water from above was diverted into the box. There was no great turbulence in the chamber, just the loud sound of the water rushing in. On the slimy sidewalls there were flush hooks for tying the boat to steady it during the operation. There were also ladders built into the walls, going way up to the top and I wondered under what circumstances one would have to climb them. Up, up we rose, imperceptibly. I cannot recall the time it took to rise the 40 feet; perhaps fifteen to twenty minutes.

Ardnacrusha chamber

When we had reached the 40-foot level, another gate opened to allow access to the second chamber; this one was more imposing as its height was 20 feet greater than the previous one. The gate closed behind us and it was awesome being inside the huge rectangular box which was getting gradually smaller as we ascended. It was like being in a massive elevator, except the floor was water. This time I knew exactly how long it took to rise the 60 feet: one and half times longer than the previous. I remember saying that to Len and he agreed, but reminded me that the rate of water flow into the chamber had to be the same for both lifts for my statement to be true. The 100-foot lift we had gone through replaced the eleven locks mentioned in the sailing directions of 1838–9.

After exiting the dam, we had four more bridges to navigate before Lough Derg – these were easy because the water level in the headrace canal was not influenced by the tides. Compared with the exacting, head-scratching, concentrative, though highly educational, couple of hours prior, it was child's play. After we refitted the mast in Killaloe, the boat's owner drove me and Len home – after a job well done.

Chapter 2

FIRST COMMAND/*Whippet*

Before moving on to *Polyanna*, the first yacht I owned, I account here for the sake of completeness, and also because it was one of my significant voyages, the circumstances of my first command, which took place not 'on the far side of the world' but on the opposite side of the Atlantic. In 1989 I was in New Jersey, USA, spending a summer holiday with cousins. A friend of the family got wind that I had done some sailing and asked me if I would do a boat delivery to her summer home in Bay Head on the Jersey shore. The boat, a 24-foot sloop, was then berthed in Piermont, NY, on the Hudson River. I found a willing crew: Tommy and Tara Duffy, cousins of mine, and an acquaintance named Josh, who had some sailing experience, and his girlfriend Kai. The trip would bring us down the Hudson with Manhattan on our port side, then on past the Statue of Liberty and thereafter into open water to Sandy Hook and on down along the Jersey shore – it sounded like quite an adventure.

I spent the days leading up to the trip buying charts and a tidal atlas for the waters in our path. The crew took care of provisioning the galley. Bunks were allotted and sleeping bags stowed. Extra fuel for the engine was canned and lashed to the guardrail. And on an intensely warm July day, with the Tappan Zee Bridge at our backs, we set off from Piermont on board *Whippet* and set course south. The river was wide and navigable and our main task heading down would be to steer clear of all the traffic travelling north and south. Ferryboats, barges, tugs, day-sailers and myriad other craft went about their daily business and I couldn't help but think that we, in our modest 24-footer, were somehow in the wrong place and encroaching on this industrious toing and froing of humanity.

At the start of our voyage we had green lush vegetation to port and starboard and moved along at a leisurely four knots. In the first hour we were getting to know the boat and how she handled; it was hard to tell at this stage as we were in the river in calm conditions. After two hours we approached the northern tip of Manhattan Island and the George

Washington Bridge lay ahead in the distance. The cityscape of New York was becoming more apparent with every mile travelled and I knew that I, and probably everyone on board, was in for a spectacular passage through the most famous city in the world. On the way downriver a gentle north-easterly wind pushed us along at a sightseeing pace and the architecture of Manhattan was overpoweringly impressive in its proximity. Each mile gave us a new perspective on the skyline. The famous buildings – Empire State, Chrysler and Woolworth – dominated. The Twin Towers were a presence from a long way off and their immensity became apparent as we approached Battery Park. For me the spectacle was wondrous and unexpected as I had no plans for such a voyage during my holiday. Josh and Tommy were good tour guides and I was lucky to have them aboard. Tara and Kai took their turns on the tiller and at some stage I realised that the trip was exceptional for all on board. There was a sense of wow to the whole thing.

Some of the logbook entries for the day read:

Dep. Piermont 13.20
George Washington Bridge 17.40
Empire State Bldg. 19.26
Statue of Liberty 20.24
Anchor west of Liberty 21.25

At a point beyond the southern tip of Manhattan, in the vicinity of the Statue of Liberty, the East River joins up with the Hudson. I looked up the East River to our north-east and saw the magnificence of the Brooklyn Bridge and marvelled at the engineering feat of the Gothic-towered masterpiece. We dropped anchor in the shadow of Lady Liberty and went ashore. We hitched a ride to the town of Elizabeth, NJ, found a friendly diner, Pete's, and feasted on grilled meats and pancakes. In a 7-eleven we picked up some packs of beer and a bottle of Seagram's 7. After returning to *Whippet*, we settled in for the night under a starry sky and the soft glow from the city lights, listening to Mary Black singing 'Once in a Very Blue Moon' on a cassette player.

Lady Liberty

Josh regaled us with stories of how he and his brother would climb all the water towers and bridges of New York City: Verrazano, Brooklyn and George Washington. We chatted into the early hours and the green Lady on the plinth was privy to all that went on aboard our little ship. We were the only boat in the vicinity of the statue and I'm not sure if we were even allowed to berth there. That was twelve years before 9/11, when the US and much of the rest of the world wasn't constantly looking over their shoulders. At eight thirty in the morning, we weighed anchor and headed for the Verrazano Narrows and its bridge, which soared over 200 feet in the air – more than enough clearance for our meagre little *Whippet*.

After the bridge we were into the lower bay and our next landmark was a point east of Sandy Hook, a long strip of land sticking out from the coast of north-eastern New Jersey like a little finger. Our bearing to the that point was 160° true and thereafter we would be going close to due south to our destination. At around one o'clock, the wind freshened from the east/southeast and the sea gradually got rougher. The tendency was for the boat to gain towards the shore and we had to tack seaward to keep clear of the coast. The boat was small so it got a bit of a battering from the increasingly large waves. We reefed the mainsail – badly, I must say – and after a while two of the grommets gave way and we had to shake out the reef and start again. It was a cause for worry having a tender spot on the main. When going about, the 'extra' crew would make room in the cockpit for whoever was manning the sheets at the time. After the manoeuvre, the bodies would line the high (windward) side again to maintain balance. The second-last tack to shore found us a bit north of Shark River, our entry point into the marina basin. The crew were in good spirits and showed no concern when the odd wave would break over the bow and make its way back to the cockpit. Josh's sailing experience was evident and he exuded a quiet confidence that made the crew as a whole feel at ease. I, too, was glad he was there. On the next tack we made the river and a half an hour later we were at a berth in a marina. We had travelled a total of 60 nautical miles. On arrival, our road crew, who were following by car, were about to issue a coastguard callout because of our missed ETA. They didn't realise that ETAs when sailing dissipate with the wind.

Chapter 3

High Seas Give *Polyanna* a Lift

There are rare times at sea when one meets conditions of wind and wave which closely resemble those from another time. On a trip south from Inishmore, one of the Aran Islands, on my first yacht, *Polyanna*, we found ourselves in the middle of a following sea that slapped our starboard quarter. The sea would rush upon us and take a swipe at our rear and then retreat as if to gather momentum for the next onslaught. This was a sea I would meet again twenty years later in a vessel (*Eibhlís*) that would take far less notice of what was happening and embrace the goings-on as playful antics. *Polyanna* was relatively small and light and while she was a competent sailing vessel in varying conditions, she could be tossed a bit in heavy seas.

Polyanna sailed into Dingle in 1992 and was immediately put up for sale by its owner, a Dutchman, who had sailed the vessel from Kilrush, through the Blasket Sound and into Dingle Bay. The owner and his lady friend had a romantic notion of sailing extensively together in the coming years, but alas the poor girl was stricken with severe seasickness in the vicinity of the Blasket Islands and the romance with the sea was shattered for her. When she stepped ashore on the boards of the newly completed Dingle marina her relief was evident.

Polyanna in the Blasket Sound

Polyanna was a four-berth chine-built yacht designed by the reputable Dutch naval architect van de Stadt. The hull was not long keel in the traditional sense but a long ballasted fin ran two-thirds the length of the vessel and ended at the rudder. The hull was plywood on solid frames and her sloop rig was proportionate and well suited to her dimensions. She sailed beautifully and was an ideal starter boat for me at the time. Once I got to know her she became an excellent single-hander as well as serving as a reasonably comfortable cruiser with crew. Her lack of full headroom below and the two tight forward berths were a drawback, but that is only in hindsight. At the time she was a joy to own and gave me many hours of adventure and fun.

Len Breewood and I had the first sail in *Polyanna* in Dingle Bay a couple of days after I took possession. One of Len's first suggestions was for me to cut a circular hole in one of the bunk lids so I could accommodate a pressure cooker and have something stewing nicely as a voyage got under way. Len liked cut-outs where distinctly shaped items could reside snugly and stay put in all weather; on a 25-foot day-sailer of his own, he had a shelf with assorted holes to fit various bottles, including one for his favourite, Gordon's Gin. Len Breewood was very helpful in the early days of *Polyanna* and expressed great enthusiasm for my venture.

On this trip south from Aran, Gerald O'Driscoll, an accomplished musician and one of the mainstays of the Skibbereen Silver Band, sailed with me for the first time, apart from a day sail in my dinghy some years previous when I was introducing a group of my students to the Dingle dolphin. On that occasion a chap called Harold was also on board and he remarked after looking around at the scenery, 'What a beautiful place – fresh, clean and unspoilt'. Then he threw an empty cigarette box over the side. Gerald looked at me and rolled his eyes to heaven. Gerald was good company and loved a bit of fun; he fitted in well with the crew, which included my brother Michael, who was a master of the one-liner and generally witty. In future years whenever he would meet Gerald he would enquire of him, 'Are you still playing the bugle?' Gerald would turn his head downwards, shake it from side to side and reply with great seriousness, enunciating every syllable, 'It is not a bugle, it is a trumpet.' In time it became an accepted and playful exchange between the two. Gerald had a lofty-sounding address: 8, 98 Street, Skibbereen. When he first told me, I asked mischievously if Skibbereen really had ninety-eight streets. The address obviously had its origin in the rising of 1798. The crew was rounded off by Aodhán Mac Gearailt who was new to sailing and undertaking his first yacht voyage. Aodhán was keenly interested in the dynamics of sailing and constantly attended to trimming the sails so the best performance was achieved. He would in later years become an accomplished sailor and skipper, leading various yachts to victory in sailing regattas.

Michael liked to fish when he was on board a boat and I gave him free rein in spite of the blood and guts which he brought to the decks. A mackerel lifted from the sea and deposited in a pot on the stove in one swoop resulted minutes later in a taste that is long savoured. Both Michael and Gerald were good hands around the cooker so the crew were always well fed. The cooker on *Polyanna* was gimballed between the confines of two bulkheads and the flimsy door to the head (the toilet) was on the opposite side and directly behind the cook of the day as he stood by his chore. I looked down several times when the boat came off a wave to port and expected to see Gerald deposited on the bowl after crashing through the head's door. Following that cruise I fitted a restraining strap like the one Len used on *An tSiocháin*.

With four crewing on *Polyanna*, living space was at a premium. I had been used to the roomy interior of *An tSiocháin* and the freedom of standing erect under her decks. One time I turned up for a cruise on *An tSiocháin* with a suitcase and got a strange look from Gearoid. Whatever about accommodating a suitcase on a 40-foot Bounty, there was no hope of finding a home for it on *Polyanna*. When living on a sailing boat, soft collapsible bags serve as your wardrobe and pillow. Yet we all managed in the little home that was *Polyanna* for a week in July of 1993. In conditions like these it brings home the realisation of all the things we can live without. We washed our socks and underwear and hung them out in the billowing wind; we brushed our teeth over a mug of water and shaved using a six-inch disc of mirror steadied in a coil of rope. Each day, when the weather allowed, the sleeping bags were slung and pegged to the guard rail for airing; often in port our little ship looked like a Chinese laundry. I had to advise the crew that any items with skid marks were to be hauled in while in harbour.

This was my first cruise as skipper of my own vessel and it brought several challenges as well as fun and adventure. I was now responsible for three other souls. When cruising with Gearoid on *An tSiocháin* as a crewman, I had certain responsibilities but Gearoid carried the burden of care for all his crew. This is what every skipper finds out the first time he commands a boat. There is a new dimension to the activity. While it can still be enjoyable and thrilling it is no longer just going for a leisurely spin on a boat. My years with Gearoid had me placed well to take over a boat on my own but apart from the seamanship and assorted sailing skills, I still had to get it right in my head.

As we headed south on 200° I was helming and Aodhán was manning the sails. Michael studied the coastline to the east, which was misting over, and Gerald busied himself below checking the rations for the next meal. By midday the coast of Clare had disappeared and the sea had increased. We were being slapped about quite a bit, though we were making fair headway under the main and working gib. Gerald would look up at me from below from time to time with an enquiring expression and I would return a worried look while pretending to chew my finger nails vigorously. This bit of levity relaxed him and me. I found myself in the middle of a large sea on a small boat and realised this was my first test as skipper and guardian. Our voyage northward from Dingle to Inishmore had been in fair weather and a relaxed mood – now there was concern, which was exacerbated by the cloak of gloomy mist and fog. For me the question of confidence arose, confidence in myself and in the boat. I didn't have GPS on board. A trailing log over the stern, which was clocking our distance travelled, became detached at some stage and got lost to the sea. This didn't help matters of navigation, of course. I could no longer accurately plot our position on the chart. My plan was to maintain the compass course we were on and at a particular time, which would be a guesstimate, change course and head east for the Shannon estuary and eventually make off Carrigaholt in Clare.

The crew were in good spirits and their apparent confidence in me buoyed up my own spirits. We were getting tired from being tossed about and wished for relief. Occasionally a large lump of green water would land in the cockpit and fill it three quarters. Thankfully it would self-drain before the next instalment arrived. Onward we slogged and at about 1600 hours, I made the decision to alter course to due east, which I hoped would take us to the estuary. I discovered after forty minutes that I was wrong. Michael spotted white water breaking ahead; we were still north of Loop Head. I put the boat back on 200°. This miscalculation of mine was worrying and a setback to morale. After a half an hour a fishing boat appeared out of the grey wall of mist and rain and we manoeuvred the boat close by to shout 'Where is Loop Head?' Gerald, who was wearing a high-spec navy-issue lifejacket (which he appropriated from his brother who was in the service) with the name *L.E. Eithne* emblazoned on the front and back, was trying to hide the name with his hand, lest the fishermen ignore our plight. The fishing boat was probably after salmon, a legal pursuit at the time, but the navy patrolled the coast to enforce the licensing regulations.

A deck hand from the fishing boat pointed his forearm south and showed us three fingers – which we took to mean three miles. A half an hour later we went back on the easterly course and soon after, the Loop and its lighthouse revealed themselves. As we approached the estuary the sky opened up and restored visibility. Luck was with us as the tide was filling into the estuary. We rode huge waves as we surfed east on a broad reach. Gerald looked back through the cabin hatch at one of the waves building behind and asked: 'John, is this ok?' I think my reply was, 'We are about to find out.'

We dropped anchor in Carrigaholt at 1800 hours and then went ashore, where I phoned my brother Anthony who lived in Kilrush. He drove us to his home, where we showered and got a hot meal. We were like four zombies around his hospitable table and later slept under his roof, which was devoid of all motion except what we imagined in our sleep. I examined my shins the following morning and found deep welts and scrapes from banging off the mainsheet horse which, in *Polyanna,* extended between the cockpit seats. These injuries were to be a constant feature while sailing in that boat. Next day we sailed the boat to Kilrush and got a new galley assistant, my niece Caríosa.

Some of our crew had to go home so I left the boat in Kilrush Marina for a few days and returned with Michael and a colleague from the college, Tom McSwiney, to sail the boat home. Tom is a very experienced sailor and I had often sailed with him in his own boat. There was always a bit of fun sailing with Tom and though he treated the activity with a certain casualness, he possessed keen sailing and navigation skills. We had a pleasant day sailing along the northern coast of the Dingle peninsula and the one-liners exchanged by Michael and Tom were fast and furious. Before we knew it we were in the Blasket Sound, one of the most spectacular spots in the universe, being pushed into Dingle Bay by a gentle breeze and a favourable stream.

Chapter 4

First Classic Boat Event

The bi-annual Glandore Classic Boat Regatta is an event I have attended since I introduced *Polyanna* to west Cork in 1994. My brother Michael sailed the boat down with me that summer. As we arrived into the harbour on a fine July morning I saw *An tSiocháin* at anchor amidst a sizable fleet of visiting boats. We dropped anchor as close as we could to my sailing 'alma mater' and rowed in our dinghy to say hello to the crew. Gearoid and two of his nephews were on board, Colmán and Seamus O'Donoghue. We boarded and had tea and sandwiches. Michael, always the stirrer, asked if there was any chance of a boiled egg. On the trip down from Dingle the previous day, Michael and I had boiled duck eggs, or 'blue bombers' as he called them, off Bray Head and I had told him about the no-eggs rule on *An tSiocháin*. We bantered and recalled good times sailing on *An tSiocháin* and made arrangements for the following day's boat race in the bay.

In the afternoon Michael and I walked round to Union Hall. After the obligatory visit to Moloney's bar we returned to Glandore. The day was scorching hot and we sat on the wall across from the Glandore Inn. The crew of *An tSiocháin* turned up and Gearoid asked Michael and I if we would have a drink. We could hardly refuse a priest, said Michael to me as Gearoid crossed the road to the inn. Several minutes later Gearoid appeared with a pint of Guinness in each hand and crossed the crowded street to us. I remember the event for particular reasons. In my account of my years sailing with Gearoid I didn't dwell much on the happenings ashore in the ports we visited. The normal format was that the crew would dine together in a restaurant ashore, have some wine or beer and generally make merry and wind down if a particular voyage had been arduous. But Gearoid didn't drink. He would join us for the meal and sometimes stay awhile longer in our company before going back to the boat. We never drank on board *An tSiocháin* apart from a glass of wine with a meal and on many of the voyages I was the only drinker on board and I would not bother having a drink for the whole trip. I sometimes told my friends, jokingly, that I went on pilgrimages with Fr Gearoid. There was no rule about consuming alcohol on board Gearoid's boat – it was never stated – but we who crewed on *An tSiocháin* knew that voyaging with Gearoid was always going to be a different experience – and one which fulfilled us in many other ways. So that day in Glandore when I saw Gearoid crossing the road with a pint in each hand, I felt strangely privileged that a man of the cloth (though Gearoid was dressed at that time in his sailing casuals) was so openly acknowledging that these two boys liked a pint of Guinness. A part of me also felt that Gearoid was saying, 'Thanks, John', for the years I had spent sailing with him.

The next day Seamus joined me and Michael on *Polyanna* for the race in the bay. We were short on crew and as *An tSiocháin* had picked up extra members that day, Seamus obligingly joined the crew of *Polyanna*. The race was a handicapped event with classes determined by boat length. It was mainly a fun event and the attending boats, mainly wooden classics, got a chance to show off their cloth and sailing skills. The day had clouded over and a fairly stiff wind and choppy sea had come up by the start of the race. We were in it for the fun. The only yacht racing I had done was on *An tSiocháin* in Fenit the odd weekday evening pre-summer. We did it for the fun then too and were probably frowned upon by the dedicated racers for whom winning was everything. All of my boats were bought with cruising in mind. That's just me; the sport of yacht racing is enjoyed by a large and enthusiastic body of seagoing boatmen.

After a time of exhaustive tacking, heeling over on our ear and getting drenched from the waves coming back over the coach roof, we eased off and opted out of the race and went for a leisurely sail for an hour. When we came ashore later the day had closed in with heavy drizzle and fog. All of the boats in the race were at anchor before us and I got vibes later that Gearoid may have been getting concerned when we were not showing up. *An tSiocháin* was in the race as well and presumably had lost track of us when we exited the race. Seamus was a college student at the time studying dentistry but he was still under Gearoid's wing, I'm sure, and may have been told off by his uncle for not letting him know, by VHF or otherwise, of our intentions. This I only surmised at the time, but if that was the case Gearoid would have been right. All three of us on *Polyanna* enjoyed that day's sailing. We had many laughs at our inefficiencies and blunders going around the buoys in Glandore Bay. Later that night

Michael and I met up with Seamus and Colmán for a couple of drinks. The two students were understandably not flush with money at the time and Michael and I probably bought an extra round or two. After the last round was deposited on the counter by Michael, Seamus chirped up, 'Good luck lads, the fillings are on me.'

Some days after the Glandore Regatta, Michael, Johnny Moloney and I sailed to Castletownshend, (Baile An Chaisleáin or 'the town of the castle'), a picturesque harbour about four miles west of Union Hall. Michael was wearing Telecom Éireann-issue steel toe-caps which were incongruous with proper yachting apparel. This brought out the scut in Johnny Moloney who sported expensive deck shoes. After lunching in Mary Ann's on our arrival we took a good look at the village, which is essentially one long steep street with a most inconvenient large tree smack in the middle of the road. The harbour setting is what makes Castletownshend. Larger boats have to anchor farther off and seeing the various craft bobbing in the harbour makes for a picture postcard setting. The background to the harbour is scenic and has some old-style buildings which exude historic vibes. The harbour is exposed to southerly winds, though there is an upper section that provides good shelter. In later years I would visit Castletownshend often and introduce it to a good number of friends and crew. The rowing regatta held there annually is an event I have seldom missed.

Chapter 5

Sailing in Dingle Bay

It was in *Polyanna* that I first started exploring Dingle Bay, which is at my back door. The bay has a thirteen-mile opening from the Atlantic Ocean, which extends from Slea Head on the Dingle peninsula to Bray Head at the western tip of Valentia Island. The eastward run of the bay is 18 miles to the dunes at Inch beach where Rosie Ryan walked and lost her parasol in *Ryan's Daughter.* Beyond the dunes the waters of the bay continue as far as the Castlemaine River where boats at one time traversed the river as far as Castlemaine Pier.

Knightstown on Valentia Island is well known to all of my boats, but it was on *Polyanna* that I first visited there under sail. A friend, John Griffin, and I would sail across regularly during the summer months and stay overnight tied up to the old pier. In later years, visitors' moorings were laid down and now a marina has been installed. The slate quarry on the island, which reopened in the late nineties, provided the slates for the British Houses of Parliament. The island was also the eastern terminus for the first viable transatlantic telegraph cable. Valentia is unspoilt in many ways and I often wonder why the place is not overrun with tourists in the summer time. The people are friendly there and the countryside provides some great scenery from several angles.

Knightstown clock

In 1970 a bridge linking the mainland at Portmagee with Valentia was completed. The design of the bridge allowed for it to pivot and allow yachts and other craft to travel the southern channel to Portmagee and onwards to exit to the south of the island. But the pivoting mechanism of the bridge has not worked for more than twenty-five years due to neglect of the mechanical workings of the bridge, which stemmed from the lack of interest in developing sailing facilities in the area. In recent years, marinas have been installed in Knightstown and Cahersiveen along with a visitors' pontoon in Portmagee, but a vital component in their viability (the bridge) has been allowed to seize up from lack of use.

As a sailor I can attest to the value of having the Valentia Bridge opening. Many a time I got a pasting going around Bray Head on voyages north and south around its headland, which is noted for the turbulent sea state that prevails regularly in its vicinity. On several trips south out of Dingle Bay from Dingle, I would wait for suitable weather conditions to round Bray Head to get it behind me while the going was good. If the bridge at Portmagee was working and allowed for a passage south of the island, the weather concerns would be lessened and there would be the attractive option of staying overnight.

Seine boat used in south Kerry regattas

Cahersiveen River was a tricky one to navigate before the marina was constructed and the channel upriver was buoyed. A strict adherence to the landmarks, which were strategically placed painted telegraph poles, was necessary. In the summertime some of the poles were indistinguishable from the profuse greenery in the background. *Polyanna* spent several nights tied up at Cahersiveen outside fishing trawlers prior to the construction of the marina there. John Griffin and I would have a meal in the town and soak in a bit of the atmosphere in Mike Murts Pub where a variety of local characters and some former students of mine like to jaw on a Saturday night. John and I did an extensive tour of the church in Cahersiveen on one of our first visits and lit candles before leaving for those who were no longer with us. Fr Gearoid would have been proud of me.

After one of our day trips home from Knightstown, John and I were telling stories in the cockpit under the dark moonless sky. I had a GPS onboard, which was turned off, and we were following a compass course for the entrance to Dingle Harbour. The night was moving on as we passed various lights on land to port on our way across the bay. After a long time I decided to go down below and turn on the GPS and found that we had long passed the entrance to Dingle harbour. We had travelled east as far as Bull Head. It turned out that Dingle lighthouse was not working that night and when we passed the entrance to Dingle we assumed we were looking at the lights of Ventry. I learned a lesson about taking my eye off the ball and the danger of assuming that lighthouses always work. We turned about and plotted a course for the harbour. Coastal radio stations issue security messages over the VHF, which contain safety messages regarding dangers to navigation. A missing light on a lighthouse would come under such a warning but since I didn't have the VHF switched on, I never heard the message.

***

Kells Bay on the southern coast of Dingle Bay is a lovely cove where one can drop an anchor and have a very relaxing few hours or go ashore in a dinghy to lounge on the sandy beach. There is quietness there and a tropical feel on a fine day which allows the mind to wander to faraway places. Ventry harbour, 5 miles west of Dingle, is large and lends to exciting sailing when the wind is brisk from the north-west. I have spent enjoyable afternoons tacking across the wide expanse of the harbour while gaining on the beach and the pier on its eastern flank, which allows for tying up at suitable tides for a sojourn in Quinn's Pub for light refreshments, then away again, goose-winging out of the harbour into the bay beyond to join the fishing boats returning with their catch.

The jewels in the crown of wonders in the periphery of Dingle Bay are technically beyond the bay. The Blasket Islands, west of Dunmore Head, which is the westernmost point in Europe, are splendid when viewed from the sea, a sight unequalled elsewhere around the coast. In addition to that, the view from the islands of the mainland is remarkable too. I have sailed through the Blasket Sound in various boats and I believe the road between the islands and the mainland provides one of the most striking vistas imaginable anywhere. The Great Blasket is the island most visited nowadays and I have anchored off its beach and gone ashore from *Polyanna* and *Eibhlís* (which will be featured in part three).

In 1995 I went on a trip to An Tearaght, the westernmost of the Blasket group, and went ashore there. The manoeuvre was tricky as we had to wait for a surge of water to raise the dinghy to the level of the landing area before alighting; the yacht in which I was sailing belonged to a friend and it stayed at anchor while the party went ashore. Three of our crew walked up to the lighthouse and we studied the granite construction that has stood for over a hundred and thirty years. The island boasts one of the oldest and the steepest funicular (sloping) railways in Europe. Our group stood in awe of what was achieved while constructing the lighthouse and its surrounding buildings in such an inhospitable place. There are still remnants of the crane that hauled materials up from the sea more than 100 metres below. I thought of Fr Gearoid telling me of the joy he and his crew experienced when seeing the light from An Tearaght flashing twice every twenty seconds as *An tSiocháin* came within nineteen miles of the island after crossing the Atlantic. On our return to Dingle, we completed a circumnavigation of the Blaskets group – a breathtaking experience. Every mile presents a vista more awesome than the one before. My own favourite is sailing through the gap between Inishnabro and the Great Blasket Island.

After four years I moved on from *Polyanna*; she went through several owners in the following ten years – one being a young Frenchman who located with the boat to Cahersiveen and undertook a major refit, giving the great little boat a new lease of life.

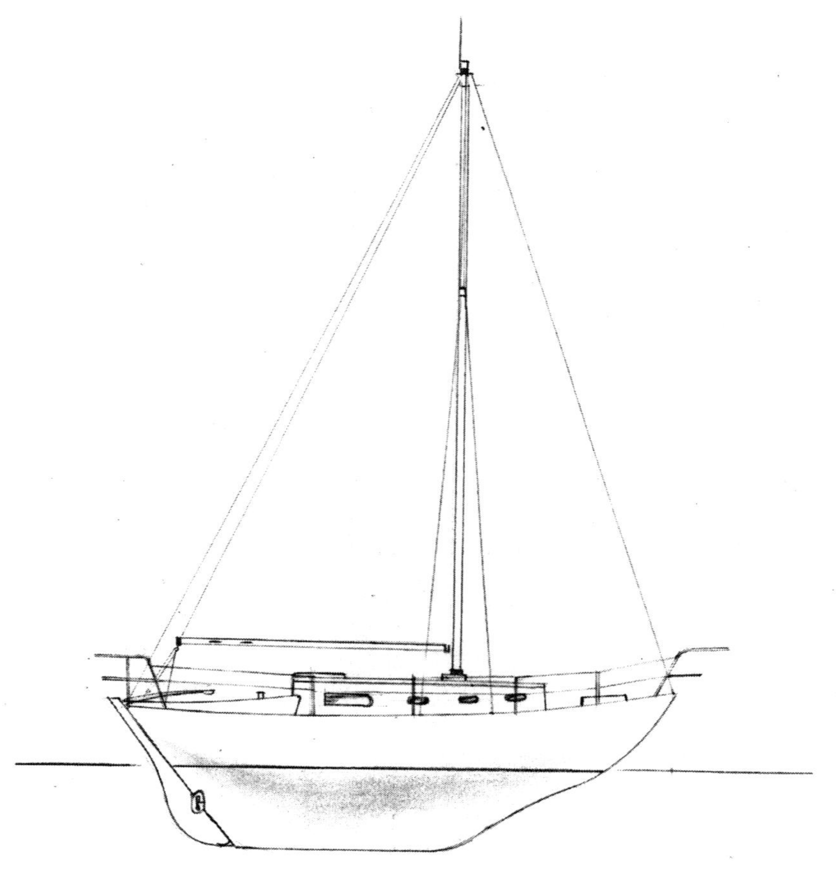

Part Three

Eibhlís

Chapter 1

SAILING *Eibhlís* HOME

The boat with the unpronounceable name, for some, and for which epithet I got my only prize ever at the Glandore Classic Regatta, *Eibhlís*, was found by me in the Hamble River near Southampton. In January of 1996, I spent a couple of days in the south of England with a friend, John Griffin, looking for the vessel which would feature in my sailing adventures in the future. She was on the hard when I inspected her and I was immediately impressed by the 'cut of her jib'. At 32 feet in length with a decent freeboard and a 5-foot draught she was eminently proportioned by the hands which first laid her out on a loft floor.

Of traditional wooden construction with good body in her bilges, which tucked in gracefully to meet her long keel, she looked every bit the classic. Her sheer line discreetly flared to her round stem-head and aft it rose deceptively to her transom, which had a hung rudder and raked aft at just the right angle, unlike the modern GRP hull transoms which rake forward and look ridiculous. Her accommodations were rich in wood furnishings and spaciously appointed, except for the bunk under the chart table, which would be designated in future voyages to the hand whose proportions suited its confines. The cockpit was roomy, with high coamings, and looked like it would give great shelter from any wind-blown wave that inclined to take up residence within. Her 'stick', as an American once called her mast, was stout and rigged sturdily to take the loads imposed by her sails when full and shrieking to come loose from a ripping wind.

I was in love. Our relationship was to last sixteen years – longer than many unions in my social orbit. *Eibhlís* was designed by renowned naval architect Alan Buchanan and built for its first owner in a boatyard in Kent in 1961. The name that came with the vessel was Eileen Elizabeth III, spoken Eileen Elizabeth the Third; though I had two aunts Eileen, and one Elizabeth, I couldn't envisage sailing into ports in Ireland with the given moniker. I sidestepped the superstitious issue of changing the name of a boat by going for a Gaelic version that embraced both names, hence *Eibhlís*. In my second year of ownership I scraped off the white paint from her topsides to reveal full-length mahogany planking (with no butt joints), which I duly oiled and varnished. Wherever I sailed with her, she got admiring glances, and I innumerable enquiries as to her provenance. She was to keep the varnished look until the year before I sold her on.

Bringing *Eibhlís* home was a big adventure for me. It was a considerable journey from the Hamble River to Dingle and it would be my first long overnighting voyage as owner/skipper – the responsibility weighed heavy on me. My crew was made up of Mark Greely, who was then recently appointed as sailing instructor to Dingle Sailing Club; and Tom Collins and Alan O'Sullivan, both students of aquaculture in IT Tralee. We spent a couple of days at the marina in Hamble getting the boat ready. When an engineer found a problem with the heater plugs in the 19hp engine, our stay had to be extended. This would subsequently result in splitting the trip into two legs. We finally got away on 12 April at 1400 hours. The weather was overcast and drizzling as we pointed *Eibhlís* towards the Isle of Wight to the south. Three hours later, past Yarmouth and the Needles, we were on our way west-southwest along the southern English coast.

During the dark of night the weather got fairly nasty. A penetrating rain and a strong wind with a rolling sea behind us had us on a most uncomfortable point of sailing. The main boom jibed at will regardless of who was on the helm – it is a point of sailing I still hate. There was no way then to secure a preventer to the boom. It relied on its weight and gravity to keep it low but with the hull bouncing from the following sea the boom constantly shifted sides. The foresail, which was on a self-tacking boom, did a similar thing to the main, though less egregiously. I had hired a life raft for the trip home and had it lashed to the top of the coach roof, but the lashing gave way during the night and we nearly lost the life raft over the side. It was the canister type which was impossible to grip when wet. It took three of us to manhandle it and coax it down below to the cabin. We did this under duress because of the swinging boom and the lashing rain.

All through the night the torment continued. I was ill-prepared for the dancing boom and silently reprimanded myself several times for not having taken this into consideration in advance. I knew that we would be getting to know the boat on the way home to a degree, but that aside, I should have been more prepared. Mark, who was experienced, and Tom, who was strong and eager to learn, were a blessing to have on board. Alan was not feeling well but he kept us going with hot drinks and food. He said to me in the early hours: 'John, I'm not feeling great but I will do anything you ask.' Such a sincere statement of loyalty was uplifting and I responded: 'Alan, we are all only doing the best we can. I'm glad to have you on board.'

The night wore on and wore us down and sometime before dawn things started to get better. In the early morning the sun shone and some hours later, in jubilant mood, we sailed past the breakwater in Plymouth Harbour and sought out a marina. As we rounded and headed for a berth, a group of onlookers were observing our weather-beaten state and one commented: 'It's nice to see a real boat coming in to the marina.' I realised that in spite of the rough night we had at sea, the integrity of the boat was never an issue. A lot of our discomfort was perhaps due to lack of preparation. *Eibhlís* had come through admirably.

During the day as we tidied up and prepared to leave the boat for a week or so, I noticed something that shook me to the core. I called Mark to share my discovery: at the bottom of the forestay turnbuckle where a through bolt secured it to the deck fitting, the nut was missing. Either we had started the journey without it or it wasn't sufficiently locked and came loose during the night. It was my responsibility as I had supervised the standing of the rigging. To think that the mast was vulnerable during the night at sea gave me pause and I realised all I had yet to learn.

That was the first leg of the first voyage of my ownership; we had travelled over 130 miles in twenty-five hours. We flew home to our onshore duties assured that *Eibhlís* was safe and secure till our return.

Ten days later I was back with a change of crew. Tom was still on board and Robin Turner completed the trio. We left Plymouth at 1900 hours and made for Newlyn in Cornwall. After ten hours of favourable overnight sailing conditions we had Lizard Point abeam at five the following morning. Three hours later we tied up at Newlyn Pier outside a fishing trawler. Our intention was to stop overnight but seeing that the weather was holding good, we decided to stock up with fuel and rations and head away during the day. I assigned shopping chores to my crew and I saw to preparations on board for the longest section of the homeward voyage.

Robin, a musician friend of mine, was meeting Tom for the first time and they got on swell. Tom is most agreeable and obliging. He fits into company easily. Robin, who generally takes getting to know and is often distracted when passing a mirror, is good to have on your side. The banter between the two crewmen was enjoyable to the ear and good for the soul. Having people on board who don't have issues or attitude problems is always pleasant. There is a note in the logbook for the date of departure that Robin spilled diesel on the deck when filling and was due twenty lashes for the offence. This was entered willingly by Tom on my command.

At two o'clock we departed from the harbour of Newlyn and motored to Land's End. The wind was negligible, a cat's paw from the south-west. Two hours later we rounded the headland where I saw familiar friends from my days on *An tSiochåin*: the Seven Stones and Longships lighthouses were to port and starboard and the Wolf was over my left shoulder. 'Put her on 308,' I called to Tom. We were going home. This was the biggy, another landmark in my sailing life. I was about to skipper a boat on my longest voyage to date – it was 170 sea miles from Land's End to Union Hall. A moderate south-westerly filled our sails after we cleared the toe of the headland. The sea was mildly ruffled. I had two good men beside me. Things were looking good.

I felt a sense that everything I had done before this, sailing-wise, was for the purpose at hand. This stretch of water, called the Celtic Sea, was familiar to me. I had sailed it with Fr Gearoid a number of times, under his command, his responsibility. There is little that weighs heavier on a person than responsibility. One's own mettle is never tested when shored up by another. When sailing along a coastline, a good sailor will have scrutinised the relevant chart for safe harbours in case emergencies of weather or other types of emergency arise. On a thirty-three-hour journey, such as we had before us, no options for diverting existed. Sailors have different ways of accommodating such voyages in their minds, I'm sure; I look to the halfway mark and think, 'There is no turning back now.'

There is a certain sense of failure in turning back; either a failure to make way in a trying sea or the failure of having misjudged the decision to head out in the first place. While the decision to return to a safe harbour may be prudent, there is still a weakening of spirit for having done so. The question didn't arise for us thankfully. We enjoyed fair weather for the entire trip. After the uncomfortable ride we had along the southern coast of England on the first leg, it was good to see the boat perform in good sailing conditions. On the way north we stowed the self-tacking jib and clipped on a light genoa. *Eibhlís* swished through the water and thumped away the small waves effortlessly. I had rigged up a temporary preventer for the boom in case we needed it but the wind stayed well on our port quarter for most of the journey.

At the halfway mark I felt a tremendous sense of elation. The phrase 'It's all plain sailing from here' came to mind. As the darkness of the second night beckoned, I estimated a landfall between eleven and midnight. As we were coming near, Robin inquired as to the onshore entertainments in Union Hall and busied himself with ablutions in front of a mirror lit up by a lantern. Tom and I had some fun on the side as we watched Robin's preparations. The darkness on the approach to Glandore Harbour was deep and had I not sailed in there on *An tSiochâin* and *Polyanna* in the past I would have been truly tested. I did have a GPS with digital readouts of co-ordinates but that information had to be applied to the chart regularly. As we neared the harbour, the lights of Glandore and Union Hall enabled me to fix exactly where I was. It was Saturday night and I knew there would be a disco and late bar in The Marine Hotel in Glandore. After checking the tides I decided to go for Glandore Pier and we tied up *Eibhlís* in her first port of call (under my ownership) in Ireland.

I stepped onto the pier and savoured the moment as if I had crossed the Atlantic. I shook hands with my crew and we walked up the pier and crossed the road to the hotel to partake of a beverage of our liking. Presently I met several of my friends from Union Hall. They gave Tom a hard time over the checked golfing-type trousers he was wearing. Robin got into the swing of the atmosphere and couldn't tell if the local tricksters were winding him up half the time or what. Tom is from Greystones, Wicklow, and that night on 27 April, would be the beginning of a long association with West Cork for him. He subsequently got a job as barman in Moloney's pub and went on to marry a local girl and take up permanent residence in the area. He would sail with me again before his commitments to married life kicked in.

Union Hall and its denizens will figure a good deal in these memoirs, but I will say here that in all the years I have been calling to the port, I, and anyone I was with, always got a great welcome. West Cork people tell us Kerry folk that we are 'cute hoors', but in reality they are the cute ones. That aside, you can always tell if you have become an adopted son or not. That night after the disco we brought *Eibhlís* round to Union Hall harbour. We were not short of crew as a half dozen from the village took the offer of a spin home on board my new acquisition. I left *Eibhlís* in Union Hall for a week and returned with my brother Michael, who would join the rest of the crew, Alan (back on board again, to my delight) and Tom to see the boat safely to her new home, Dingle.

Chapter 2

Eibhlís's Fastest Spin/Oileán Chléire

In July of 1996, *Eibhlís* sailed south again as far as Kinsale. Tommy Duffy, who sailed with me aboard *Whippet*, was visiting Dingle for a few weeks and was delighted to have the opportunity to sail in Ireland. Michael and Nicholas Hawes (our nephew) were also on board. We stopped off in Valentia, Oileán Chléire and of course Union Hall. We also introduced *Eibhlís* to her first parade of sail in Glandore. In Kinsale we were rafted outside a visiting motor yacht, which had well-maintained brightwork, and as we crossed its deck to get to the pontoon we were requested by a portly gentleman not to step on his varnish. Nicholas looked at me and I at Michael. Tommy looked at all of us and he asked me as we walked towards the gangway if that guy was for real. We enjoyed a good meal ashore and had a bit of fun.

On returning to Union Hall I met Seamus O'Donoghue, who was sailing in a boat named *Second Wind* with some friends. Seamus and Fr Gearoid (as captain), along with three others, had sailed on *Second Wind* the previous year when it crossed the Atlantic from Baltimore (USA) to Fenit. Their crossing, which took in Chesapeake Bay and Cape May and had them in three days of fog around the Grand Banks and strong gales in mid-Atlantic, took twenty-eight days. Two weeks out from Ireland, *Second Wind* contacted the Concorde (flying from London to NY) via air-band and spoke to its captain, who relayed messages to the families of the seafaring crew that all was well.

My crew travelled home by road and I left *Eibhlís* in Union Hall and cruised to Dingle on *Second Wind*, taking in Oileán Chléire, Schull and Long Island. While in Dingle we did a day trip to the Blasket Islands and had Kay (who sailed with me on *An tSiocháin*) on board and a mutual friend Gráinne, who, in spite of not always feeling well at sea, endured the discomfort for the chance to have an adventure and a bit of fun. We anchored off the beach at An Blascaod Mór and had lunch on board under a clear blue sky. There was a bit of a roll in the sea and food was not on top of the list of enjoyments for all on board.

Seamus and I exchanged sailing stories as we did when we met. I would say something like: 'When I was sailing my boat home from England, such and such …' Seamus would come back with: 'Well, when I was crossing the Atlantic …' It was enjoyable one-upmanship banter. Seamus's offerings were presented humbly with a mischievous glint in his eye. A couple of years later Seamus would outdo me completely after sailing round the world in *Second Wind*. More about that to come.

After spending five days on *Second Wind*, I returned to Union Hall and made plans to bring *Eibhlís* home. In early August on a fine calm day, I departed from Union Hall alone and headed for the Mizen and northward. Six hours later, with Crookhaven abeam, I heard the sound of the engine change and a rattling sound beneath my feet. I lifted up the hatch in the cockpit sole and saw a flow of water coming in around the stern tube. On closer inspection I saw that the tube had come loose and that with increased throttle, the water rushed in faster. I suspected that the propeller had lost a blade and created an imbalance, which loosened the stern gear. I recalled the degraded state of the two-blade propeller when I checked out the boat in Hamble and thought at the time that I would get the season out of it – and I almost did. A worry for boat owners is electrolytic corrosion – the decaying of the least noble metal when a number of metals are in contact with water, which acts as an electrolyte. Simply put, the weakest metal will corrode and at the stern of a boat underwater there are normally three or four different metals acting out this unseen scenario: stainless steel, brass or bronze and a sacrificial metal like zinc, which needs to be replaced regularly in order to preserve the others.

I stuffed some cloth into the gap between the flange and the deadwood and re-tightened the coach screws. After applying some throttle, even at low revs, the water flowed again. There was no wind, so rounding the Mizen was out of the question. Crookhaven was close by. I would have to limp in there somehow. After an hour of low revs and tightening the screws every ten minutes, I was outside the entrance to the harbour. There I hailed an inbound small fishing boat and got a tow in to a mooring and later, at high tide, to the slipway by the pier where I dried out *Eibhlís*. At low water I got underneath the hull and found that there was a blade missing from the propeller. I considered my options, which were not good. I tightened the tube inside and out and stuffed mastic between the flanges, knowing that if I started the engine and engaged the shaft my work would be undone again. Getting in and out of Crookhaven by road to the nearest chandlery in the hope I could get a new propeller was a daunting prospect. I decided to get a tow out of the harbour the following morning and hope for wind to get me home. For a fee, I was deposited in the outer bay the next day. I put up every bit of cloth the boat could carry. The wind was less than slack and variable in direction and I sailed towards the Mizen several times only to end up where I started again later. Towards evening I had made some ground eastwards towards Oileán Chléire and thought that would be the better option as night would soon be approaching. I saw the *Naomh Ciarán II* ferry making its last run of the evening into the island and hailed Conchubhair, the ferry operator, on the VHF radio and explained my situation. He told me to stand by and he would come alongside and throw me a towline. After tying up to the ferry, *Eibhlís* got the fastest spin of her life behind the ferry to the entrance to North Harbour. Doing about fourteen knots I was a spectacle and a bonus attraction for the passengers who were on board. After arriving at the pier I was helped into the inner harbour where I tied up to the pier wall, glad to be in for the night.

It would be dishonest to put forth a record of my travels whereby all the places I've visited came out smelling like roses. Thankfully, in the majority of the places I sailed into, my crew and I were welcomed warmly and given assistance as a matter of course whenever needed. I cannot say that of Crookhaven. I am not enamoured with the place. The previous year when I was in there with *Polyanna*, I was charged for leaving a couple of ice packs in the fridge of a local hostelry overnight, after my crew and I had spent quite a bit of money there during our stay. Apart from that incident, I never felt at home there. There is also an eager promptness in collecting the fees for harbour moorings as soon as a boat puts its snout into the harbour. While sailing around Ireland a number of years later I never had to pay for a visitor's mooring. So it was ironic that *Eibhlís* got into difficulty outside the harbour I least wanted to visit.

This is an opportune time to relate some of the experiences I have had in Oileán Chléire, our southernmost island, situated off the coast of west Cork. I have connections with the place in two regards. My sister-in-law Mairéad hails from the island and is a sister of Conchubhair from the ferry mentioned above. Conchubhair is now sadly deceased. I also have two former students from the island, Mick Donoghue and Michael Cadogan. On various voyages I would stop overnight with my crew and meet up with the locals in Club Cléire on the harbour's edge where a nice homely atmosphere prevailed. There, Conchubhair and I would exchange news of our respective abodes over a few drinks. He had a huge store of local knowledge and was very helpful to me in my early days cruising the grounds around Long Island Bay and the Gascanane sound; once he bade me follow the ferry through the north entrance to Baltimore so I would become familiar with its narrow gap. Conchubhair was respected and well liked on the island and throughout west Cork. He left a huge gap in the social fabric of the island when he died in 2004.

Mick Donoghue would assist me in any way he could during my visits and I remember one night when I stayed over in Michael Cadogan's house, I was kept awake by the swish of light from the Fastnet Lighthouse, which passed my bedroom window every five seconds. On recounting this to Michael the following morning I got the rejoinder: 'What light? We don't notice that anymore.' The island is noted for its steep inclines and the cars that navigate them while groaning under the pressure. One can always tell when somebody is coming to town by the loud and exhaustive announcement which can be heard from a long way off. There is otherwise a calmness and secluded feel to the island. It is a place where one will be left alone if so desired but where there is also the feeling that help is always at hand. Since I started sailing south from Dingle, scarcely a year has passed that I have not called to experience the welcoming embrace of the harbour and its people.

I have digressed from my earlier explanation of the means by which I entered the harbour on that early August day in 1996. After tying up at the inner pier I cooked a very welcome meal, which I had partly prepared during the day while I was lolling about in the bay. Afterwards I naturally headed to Club Cléire for a drink with Conchubhair and told him of my plan, which was to leave *Eibhlís* tied up and go overland to Dingle and get the necessary tools and equipment to effect a repair by the pier on my return. My boat was in the safest possible place until I would return and I had plenty of friends who would keep an eye on her in my absence. So I took the ferry to Baltimore the next day and made my way home to gather the kit I needed. Eight days later I returned with my godson Alan from Dunboyne, Co. Meath, who was visiting me for a week. He could not have arrived at a better time. We got the repairs done between tides and *Eibhlís* not only departed Oileán Chléire with a new three-blade propellor, but a brand new stern tube and all necessary fittings. As we left the harbour her new prop chewed the water with vigour and churned up a brand new wake. There was no wind and we steamed all the way home, arriving in Dingle marina thirteen hours after we set out.

Chapter 3

Soft Landing in Truro

When getting my notes together for this chapter I pulled out the chart of the Fal River on which I have circled a cross marking where *Eibhlís* went aground in the mud a half mile from Truro, Cornwall, in 1997. The co-ordinates of the spot accompany a note describing the circumstances of the ignominious event. I compared my chart with Google Maps so I could see exactly, from the air, where *Eibhlís* struck. Seventeen years later (as I write) I am in awe of the technological advances that now aid the yachtsman. I did have GPS then, but it was basic with a digital display showing co-ordinates that had to be transferred to the paper chart. When sailing alone in a confined channel where you cannot deviate from your compass course for very long, it is extremely trying if too many things need doing at once. With the aid of Google Maps, I can now see that I was tempting fate in trying to make off Truro, but it was and is possible with the right tidal window.

My error was departing from Mylor Marina, about two miles north of Falmouth, too late. The tide was rising but I underestimated the time it would take me to get through the winding river Fal, which became the Truro river further north, to the town of Truro. About a half mile from Truro, the tide had started turning, and though the river was marked with single buoys at varying intervals, I cut a corner too close and struck the soft mud. A small boat with two fishermen came along and tried to pull me off but the tide was falling too fast and after ten minutes I asked the two Cornishmen to abandon their effort. I stayed with the boat until she had dried out completely at about three in the afternoon. Then I donned a pair of wellies and slung my walking shoes around my neck. I also lowered the dinghy on to the mud and dragged it to shore. The mud was soft and several times when I raised my leg I left a wellington behind in its sucking grip. I made the shore, tied the dinghy to a farm gate and walked across the fields to Truro.

Eibhlís in the mud

I was in the mood for a drink and lo and behold didn't I find an Irish pub to have it in. The said establishment also served a good Irish stew, which went down a treat. While *Eibhlís* was falling over in the mud, the angle of the galley didn't lend itself to cooking a decent meal. I relaxed for an hour and thought over the voyage that brought me to where I sat. Ten days previous I had departed from Dingle with Mark (back on board again, always welcome), my nephew Nicholas, on his first long trip, and Liam Long, who would become a constant sailing companion over the following fourteen years. We had fair weather going south and made Oileán Chléire in less than twelve hours, where we stayed overnight and celebrated Liam's birthday. It was the fourth of July. On the next leg the following day we flew the spinnaker after exiting the Gascanane Sound and kept it filled all the way to High Island where we turned off for Union Hall.

We took the ground at the old pier in Union Hall and asked Nicholas to stand watch that night lest we miss the tide in the morning. He paced the sandy beach throughout the starlit night, fearful that he would fall asleep. When I awoke the next day *Eibhlís* and her full complement was fifteen miles south of Union Hall. It was the first and only time I didn't have the conn as we left harbour. The *Naval Shiphandler's Guide* states: 'One person gives orders to the ship's engine, rudder, lines and ground tackle. This person is said to have the conn.' I never asked who had the conn that morning but nevertheless we were on our way without incident apart perhaps from Johnny Moloney's veiled attempts to throw us off course the night before so we would linger longer under his wing.

At midnight we crossed the median line between Ireland and England and fourteen hours later we tied to a mooring in Hugh Town in St Mary's, one of the Isles of Scilly. During our time there we met up with the crew of *Tailte*, a naval training yacht which was anchored beside us. In the afternoon the next day we set sail for the fishing town of Newlyn in Cornwall, which was an eight-and-a-half-hour trip. There we found a Star Inn Bar (just like in Dingle) with a friendly crowd and were made so welcome that we got a 'lock-in'. The next day we walked to Penzance, which is only over the road, and did some shopping. Penzance is a fair-sized town and has a marina, which is locked and accessible for a time on either side of high water. I had covered this ground before on *An tSiocháin* with Fr Gearoid. We decided on an evening departure from Newlyn and set sail for Plymouth, which would be the easternmost extremity of that voyage, at 1930 hours. At around midnight we had a power failure off Lizard Point. All the navigation lights and instruments were down. The beam from the Lizard Lighthouse would swoop by intermittently as Liam traced the fault – a loose electrical connection. While Liam was at work, we made do with torches. We were well off the headland and clear of any dangers.

At 1100 hours we berthed at a marina in Plymouth. In the logbook the price of the overnight berth is noted: £12.80. We ate ashore and made plans. Mark and Liam were getting off in Plymouth as planned and going overland to London to meet friends. On 10 July, Nicholas, now promoted to first mate, and I sailed *Eibhlís* west along to Falmouth. After seven hours of good sailing we dropped anchor at Falmouth Yacht Haven. We had a meal in the Slow House and a few beers in the Chain Locker – Nicholas wasn't really drinking then. Nick is pleasant company and good fun to be with. He possesses a particular, endearing wit and can summon a hangdog look at will if he thinks chastisement is in the offing. He is good at sea, holds a course well in any weather and above all he gets on great with people and they with him. Unfortunately Nick had to head for home from Falmouth, so he got on the train for Swansea next day to make the ferry for Cork. After walking Nick to the train station I found myself a long way from home, alone with *Eibhlís*. I decided to do some exploring in the vicinity of the Fal River.

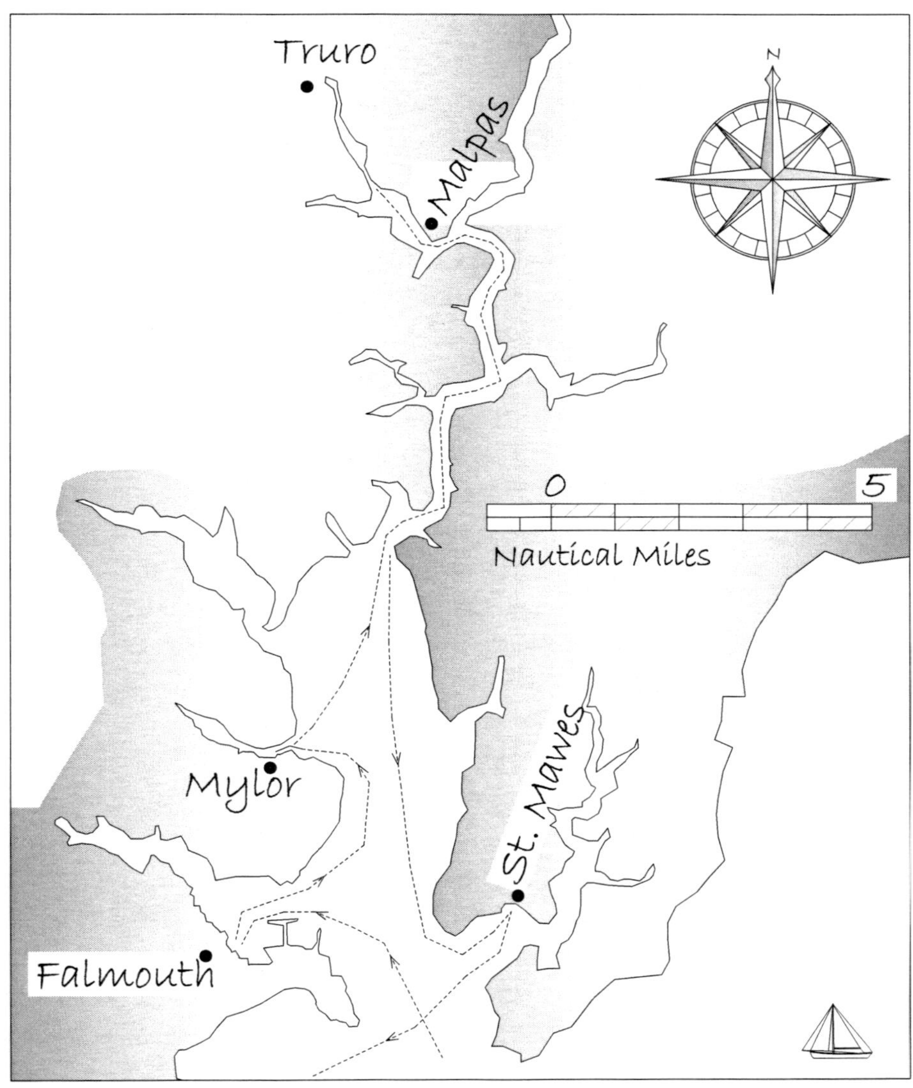

I sailed a short distance north from Falmouth to Mylor Churchtown and picked up a visitor's mooring. Mylor was quieter with a lot less traffic than the port of Falmouth. I dined ashore in the HMS Ganges restaurant and the place certainly knew how to charge – but the food was good. From Mylor I set off the following morning along the snaking river to Truro. On the way north, various creeks branched off from the main thoroughfare of the Fal River and at a small marina at Malpas the river turned to Truro. The rest of this journey and its unexpected termination I have already described.

After leaving the Irish pub, I had a look around Truro and found it to be a sizeable town – actually I discovered that it was classed as a city and that it once had a thriving port. The city has a significant cathedral and a lot of Georgian and Victorian architecture. Truro prospered greatly from tin mining in the eighteenth and nineteenth centuries. It appeared to be a busy retail city with all the modern shops of the day and, like many such cities, it retained an old and historic section.

I had calculated earlier that darkness would be approaching when *Eibhlís* was afloat again and I was reluctant to be going downriver in the dark in case I grounded anew. I remembered seeing an old barge at anchor in a pool of water on the way upriver, about a half mile from where I struck. It was my plan to reach the barge and tie up alongside it for the night. When I got back to the boat around seven thirty, the water was lapping at her bilges. I rowed out in the dinghy and clambered aboard on the low side and waited. At a few minutes past ten I started the engine and coaxed *Eibhlís* out of the mud and into the channel. As planned, about twenty minutes later I was tied up safely outside the old barge, whose name, *Trevelva,* was ghosted over with rust. Before going to the bunk I had a glass of wine as I filled in the details of my adventure in the Fal River thus far.

Early next morning, being fortified with Cornish bacon and eggs I had bought the day before, I made a leisurely wake sailing downriver as far as Malpas, where I dropped anchor. I got a bus to Truro as I wanted another good look at the place. I treated myself to a night ashore in Truro and stayed in an old-style bed and breakfast. With all of my bodily ablutions taken care of and another Cornish breakfast under my belt, I sailed south the next day for Saint Mawes, a large natural harbour, which was popular with seagoing and land-travelling tourists, a mile across the channel from Falmouth.

As can be deduced from this account, in the last five days I didn't put up much mileage as the cluster of places I visited were on the Fal estuary or upriver from it. However, they were leisurely days and the sun shone for their duration. On 16 July I left the Fal estuary behind, eager to put wind in my sails again. I had a good sail as far as the Lizard and thereafter I motor-sailed to Newlyn and tied up outside a fishing trawler by the pier. In total, it was an eight-hour trip from Malpas. Once settled in Newlyn I considered my options. I was about thirty-four hours' sailing from the south of Ireland. I made a phone call.

Barry O'Riordan, from Wicklow, studied in the IT in Tralee and was a student of mine for two years. He, along with some of his classmates and my colleague Len Breewood, helped with the setting up of the Dingle sailing club in 1987. Barry had a background in sailing and was a valuable asset when it came to giving instruction to novice sailors. We didn't always see eye to eye, Barry and me – it was a personality thing – but I knew that if I asked him for help he would respond favourably if his circumstances allowed. To cut the story short, Barry and his brother Declan arrived in Penzance two days after the phone call. We left Newlyn at 1515 hours on 18 July and enjoyed a good crossing to Union Hall where we tied up after more than thirty-five hours at sea. Barry and Declan had taken over the running of the boat on the way home and I by and large relaxed. It was good having a reliable crew on board again.

I stayed in West Cork for another ten days, sailing locally and calling to various rowing regattas in which Finbar Moloney was a keen contender. My brother Michael sailed *Eibhlís* back to Dingle with me in late July. They have a saying in Union Hall that goes: 'When John O'Connor sails home from west Cork, the summer is over'.

Chapter 4

LIFE IS A CAMARET

Eibhlís's first trip to Brittany from Dingle was exciting, especially for me as I would be covering old ground from my days on *An tSiochháin*. My crew consisted of old reliables: Mark and Tom Collins, who had sailed *Eibhlís* home from Hamble with me, and Liam Long, who would become a regular crewman in the future. Before I continue with this chapter I should devote a few paragraphs to Liam, whom you will encounter often in this work.

At the time Liam owned Long's bar in Holy Ground, Dingle. Tom Long was the name over the door. That was Liam's father. Liam had to arrange for his bar to be managed whenever he was away and once that was covered he was eager to set sail. Liam would become a regular occupier of the starboard bunk amidships in the cabin. At the end of a voyage several of his belongings, including sleeping bag, sunglasses, lifejacket, would remain on board in his quarters until the following year's trip. There were two named bunks on *Eibhlís*: the Captain's and Liam's and anyone who occupied Liam's while he was not on board knew they would have to vacate as soon as his imposing frame appeared at the companionway. I'm sure that when *Eibhlís* left my ownership there were various bits left from Liam's occupancy stuffed between the ribs at the waterline and beneath the bunk lids he slept on during over a dozen voyages.

Liam had spent a number of years fishing and was no stranger to boats, though yachting was a somewhat different kettle of fish. He soon got to know how things worked and became a skilful and reliable hand. He wasn't afraid of weather and was well able to hold a course on the tiller, even when the weather-helm threatened to tear his shoulder from its socket. His competency above deck was matched by the work he did at the cooker below in the galley. The meals he cooked on the two-ring cooker were varied, challenging to produce and sometimes experimental, but always delicious. I was probably the best-fed captain on the western seaboard. He would approach the preparations for the meal humbly, saying, 'It's just a bit of this and a sprinkle of that', etc., but what came out of the pan at the end was haute cuisine. I often wondered how he and Len Breewood would have got on in the same ship; like a kitchen on fire perhaps.

Liam and I would do several solo trips. His son Tom and his daughter Sarah would often sail with us as well. After a time Liam would take new charges under his wing and show them the ropes. I always felt more at ease when he was on board. Besides, it freed me up to do odd jobs around the boat, attend to navigation, do a bit of reading and have the odd nap. Liam's knowledge of animal life and the flora of the land was impressive. We had interesting nature walks on all of the islands, from Inishbofin to Oileán Chléire, I was lucky to have my own David Attenborough on board as we explored the seas and its coves. Any bird that flew over us was identified and any fish that broke through the waves was named. The phosphorescence beneath the bow at night that looked like crème de menthe was explained by Liam, as was the correct method of handling fish on a line before throwing them back in the water. His store of knowledge was diverse.

On the way to West Cork, my normal staging point before going south, Nicholas was on board and jettisoned (I jest, of course, Nick) in favour of Tom Collins before we departed from Union Hall at 1400 hours, being gently moved along by a moderate north-westerly wind. Later in the day the wind increased and *Eibhlís* clocked up her fastest ever speed between Union Hall and St Mary's in the Scilly Isles. In twenty-six hours we had covered the distance for which the average on future trips would be thirty hours. We stayed a night on the Scillies and left at 1120 hours the next day. Our course from the Scillies was 145° true and this took us between Ushant and its outlying islands to the west and Pointe St Mathieu on the north-west coast of France. Again we had a favourable wind and tied up in Camaret in Brittany at 1240 hours the next day, another good performance by *Eibhlís*.

Camaret is a fair-sized town with a marina and some beaches and is situated about 10 miles from Pointe St Mathieu. The day after our arrival was wet and dreary and the crew took to an extensive exploration of the town's taverns, hence the title of this chapter. Thankfully the next day we had sunny weather and a moderate north-easterly wind to push us round the Raz de Sein and on to Audierne, where after a brief stopover we left for an eight-and-a-half-hour journey to Concarneau. There is a walled island in the middle of the harbour basin that contains the old town of Concarneau. The modern town, with a population of around 20,000, is on the mainland. I was very impressed with the place. A drawbridge gives access to the Ville Close – the walled town – where a very interesting fishing museum is housed. The port itself has a large fishing fleet, so naturally we, being from Dingle, had to walk the pier and check out the local craft.

On the seafront there was a selection of bars and cafés, where we sampled good food and respectable French wine. On the night before we left we had an enjoyable sing-song with some locals in one of the haunts we had discovered. The next day we sailed merrily on a short four-hour trip west to Loctudy. While we were breakfasting on croissants and coffee at the marina in Loctudy, a neighbouring yacht, while making to leave, whacked the stern of *Eibhlís* and broke her flagstaff. The owners were apologetic and it transpired that their yacht lost steerage when the propeller came loose and buried itself on the seabed. Tom volunteered to dive under and attempt to locate the errant prop. He was successful and we got two bottles of wine for our boat as a result. The log of the event reads: 'minus one flagstaff, plus two bottles of wine'.

An eight-hour journey the next day found us back in Audierne. Our intent was to make off Morgat farther north but there was a very strong north-westerly blowing. As soon as we anchored in Audierne, a boat carrying three customs officers came alongside. One officer dived under the hull checking for attached contraband and another came aboard and checked our passports – he was an amiable fellow and asked us about stuff in Ireland. Before he left us he partook of a glass of wine. We later shopped in a supermarket for wine to bring home as gifts. We also had an order to fill for the mayor of Union Hall, Johnny Moloney.

At 1520 on 8 July, we left Brittany behind and headed for home. Tom insisted on giving Liam a break from the galley and prepared the evening meal. My crew and I eagerly awaited the results of Tom's industry at the cooker while seagulls overhead circled with similar anticipation. It, and I use this pronoun deliberately, finally arrived in the cockpit to dubious looks from Mark and Liam. I harboured similar misgivings, but as captain, I had to give Tom the benefit of the doubt. However, in the end I, too, had to concede that Tom be kept away from the cooker for the duration of the voyage. At first we were judicious in the way our spoonfuls were chucked over the side when Tom wasn't looking. After a time we abandoned all politeness and got rid of the gooey paste openly. Suffice it to say that the gulls, at least the skinniest of them, ended up with the spongy mixture of decimated pasta and anyone's guess at what else the dish contained.

During the voyage, the weather turned hardy with strong winds from north-northwest and disturbed seas. At one stage I reefed the main and put up a smaller jib, which Mark called a hankie. The crew was very much at ease with the conditions, while I, wearing the skipper's cap, could seldom relax fully. Thirty-three hours after our departure, we anchored in St Mary's. It had taken six hours longer on the return journey.

The shipping forecast for the following days for the Lundy and Fastnet areas was for gale-force winds from NNW. Mark had commitments at home and could not wait out the bad weather so he left for home by ferry to Penzance and onward by flight. We were anchored in the southern harbour off Hugh Town and there was an unpleasant roll in the sea, which made for uncomfortable nights in the bunk. During our extended stay we covered a bit of ground checking the place out. Of course I had seen it all before when I was there on *An tSiocháin*. On one of our walks we came across the Lock, Stock and Barrel pub in Old Town. The place had a pool table and we passed a good few hours there. After four days, the wind eased off sufficiently for us to take a shot at going home. We made good time on the way home. Liam and Tom were getting well used to *Eibhlís*. It was Tom's third time crossing the Celtic Sea with me. On 16 July, we tied up at Union Hall Pier.

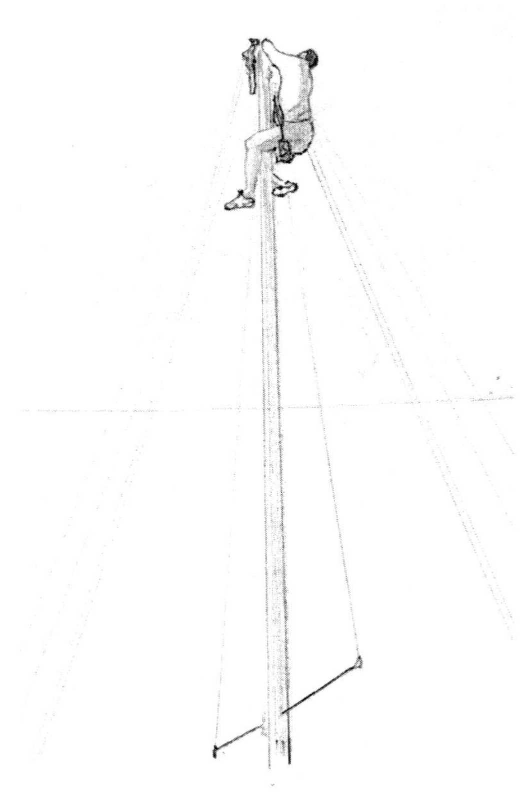

Tom aloft

On the trip back to Dingle, some days later, the most memorable event was racing up the bay from Bray Head to Dingle before a gale. On the way north I listened to the forecast every three hours and around Puffin Island the gale was 'imminent', a word only ever used by weather forecasters when things are about to get worse. Sunshine is never 'imminent' in their parlance. I was glad to be around Bray Head and into the bay before the south-westerly intensified. The logbook entry for the crossing reads: 'bumpy ride up Dingle bay'.

When I was unloading the wine, which was stored under the bunks for the long trip home, I found that most of the labels had peeled off the bottles because of the bilge water slushing about when the boat was heeled over. It was impossible to tell the plonk from the expensive stuff. Such is life.

Chapter 5

Sailing Round Ireland

In June of 1999 *Eibhlís* set off from Dingle on a round-Ireland voyage. The crew included Liam Long, his daughter Sarah and Mark Greely. In moderate westerly winds we sailed through the Blasket Sound and set course for Kinvara in County Galway. During the night there was a cold rain that lasted for a number of hours. The sweep of the light from Loop Head kept us company as we sailed north-east along the Clare coast. Sarah was feeling poorly from seasickness for most of the night and we all felt for her. At 1800 hours the following day we arrived in Kinvara harbour. It's a tidal harbour and I moved as close to the town as I thought prudent before dropping anchor. In the morning I found that my calculations were a bit off; we were stuck in about a foot of mud but were still relatively upright. *Eibhlís*, with her robust iron ballast keel, will sink into the mud and remain vertical so long as there is water under her round bilges.

While breakfasting ashore we discussed our next move. Sarah was not keen on going on with the trip. The sloppy night on the way up had taken its toll on her and naturally we were not surprised by her decision. Mark, who would have been returning home in a couple of days anyway, decided to accompany Sarah home on the bus later that day. That was agreeable to Liam and he was happy to know that Sarah would have company on the way home. Liam and I savoured the delights of the picturesque village for a couple of hours. The village has a colourful look about it with the shopfronts well kept and maintained. The pier had a Galway Hooker, *Bád Mór*, tied up alongside. This is the traditional fishing boat used in Galway bay. A smaller version from the family of Hookers, the *Pucán*, nudged at the stern of the larger boat like a small child looking for attention. The *Gleoiteog* and the *Leathbhád* complete the range of these boats whose origin date back to the mid-nineteenth century. Some of the vessels in existence are over a hundred years old and new ones are still being constructed. Every year Kinvara hosts 'Cruinniú na mBád', a celebration of the boats and the part they have played in the commerce between the islands and the mainland.

Kinvara Harbour

Around midday Liam and I sailed for Kilronan on Inishmore, one of the Aran Islands. Once we got out into Galway Bay, we sailed at a constant six knots on a port tack from a steady southerly wind. After five and a half hours of leisurely sailing we dropped anchor in Kilronan Harbour. Liam cooked up a meal of boiled potatoes, lamb cutlets and assorted vegetables and we dined al fresco. We then brought the boat alongside the pier, outside a fishing boat, and stocked up with fresh water. The next day we explored the island. At the pier head there were horses and traps, minivans and bicycle-hire stalls offering the tourists who came off the ferry tours of the island. There was a pungent smell of horse dung in the air from the horses that were idling while waiting for a fare. We extricated ourselves from the hubbub and set off for Dun Aengus (Dún Aonghasa) on foot.

Dún Aonghasa

On arriving at the cliff-top fort, which consists of four concentric walls on a plateau that is more than 100 metres above the sea, we were taken in by the breathtaking vista. It was a day of good visibility and to the south-east the coast of Clare was clear as far as the Cliffs of Moher. To the west the vastness of a shimmering sea was laid out before us. Liam, as always, studied the flora of the area and pointed out the more interesting features of the terrain. In the evening we sampled a pint or two in the American Bar and remarked on the incongruity of the name of the inn with the culture of the island. At least the giant McDonald's 'M' was nowhere to be seen.

Inishbofin, (derived from the Irish, Inis Bó Finne) off the coast of Connemara, Galway, was our next port of call, a ten-hour sail from Kilronan in the relatively light winds which were settling over the area. We spent time along the way making 'baggy wrinkles' – strands of old rope laced together for attaching to the aft shrouds to prevent chafing of the mainsail when it was fully out. There was some fierce laughter when we held a completed 'baggy' up to our chins to imitate a scraggy beard.

Skipper wears a baggy-wrinkle

Liam was good at rope work and did any necessary splicing and whipping to the lines that worked the boat. I kept the log for each day and noted the tides and tidal streams pertaining to our position at the time. I also noted details of weather forecast times and of coastguard radio operating channels. When visibility suited, we navigated from headland to headland, though noting the relevant compass bearing in the log. Occasionally we checked the GPS to check our SOG (speed over ground). On this trip I had also brought a handheld GPS as a back-up to the fixed instrument in the cabin. It would prove its usefulness later in the voyage.

Our course from Inishmore took us outside the myriad islands and rocks strewn to the west of the Connemara coast, then to Slyne Head and outside High Island, west of Aughrus Point, and on to the picturesque harbour of Inishbofin. Gearoid had introduced me to the island in the eighties and as I picked up the leading beacons, the computer chip in my brain gathered the 'bits' which it knew were there and rounded them up in a flash. We anchored off and had a meal in the cockpit. It was Liam's first time in the island and he was well pleased with the surroundings. Later on shore we checked out the lay of the land. There were some fine clean beaches in the harbour environs. As it was Liam's birthday (4 July), we made for the pub on the harbour front and each of us had a brandy and port followed by a few chasers. This would be the farthest north we would celebrate Liam's birthday while cruising on *Eibhlís*. The furthest south was Concarneau in Brittany the previous year and before that in Oileán Chléire in 1997. On subsequent trips we would be in Bear Island, Union Hall, and once more in Brittany, upriver from St Malo in a place called Dinan. The event became a fixture on our sailing calendar for a good number of years.

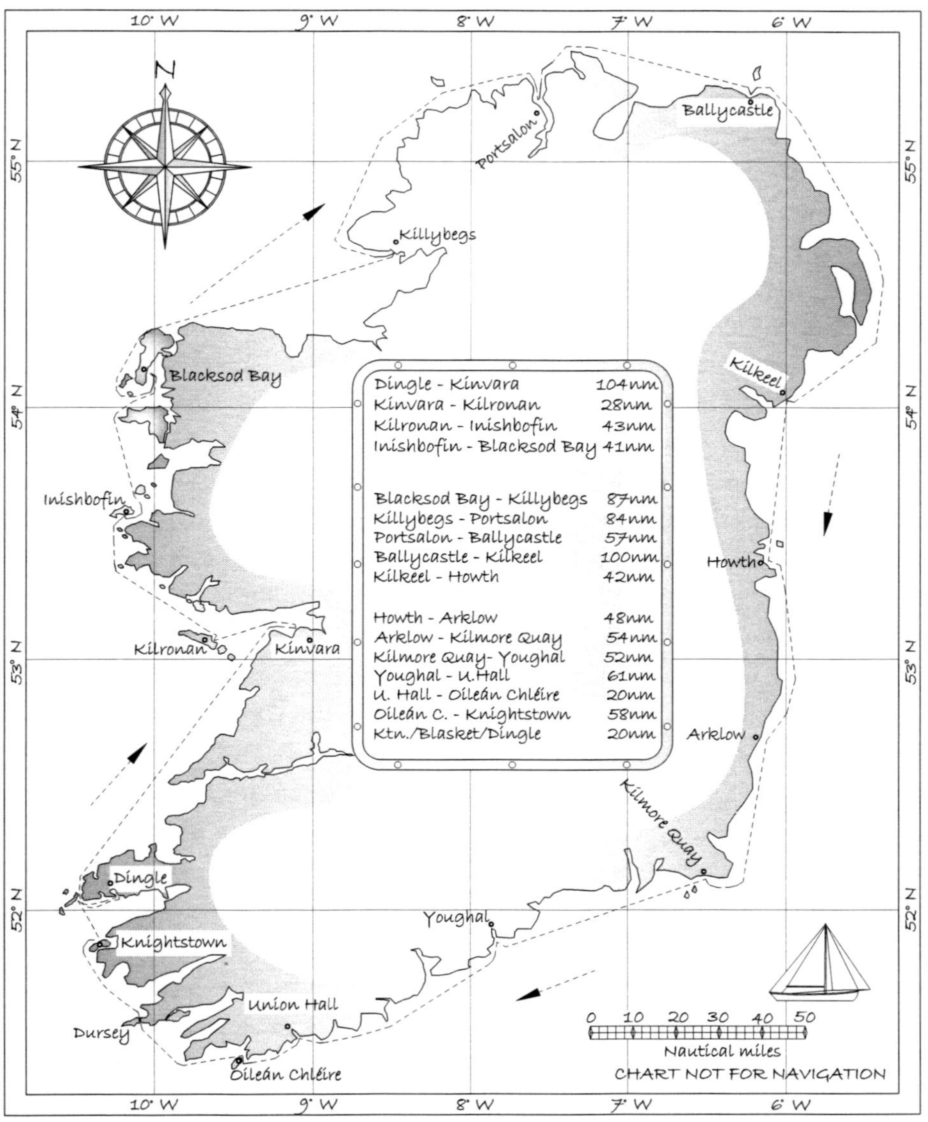

We talked with some local people in the pub. They were very welcoming and offered us showers if we needed them. I was reminded of a college friend of mine who used say: 'I shower once a month whether I need to or not.' After going back to the boat we had a snack and a glass of wine and planned the next day's cruise. This would be the norm for the entire trip. When I set out from Dingle I had no definite plans beyond Inishbofin – that was as for north as I had sailed on *An tSiocháin* – so Liam and I would be making it up as we went along from there. In order to move us on a sizeable distance each day, we tried to plan hops of around ten hours, but that didn't always hold for several reasons: wind direction and strength, suitable harbour anchorages and the need for provisioning the boat with fresh produce and fuel. On the west and north-west coasts calm weather was forecast and consequently we would be using a lot of diesel for the engine.

While rounding Inishbofin on the eastern side the next day, I looked east towards the entrance to Killary Fjord, which was ten miles off, and felt drawn to the place. It had been nine years since I sailed there on *An tSiocháin*, but now we had gained momentum for going north and we motored on. We motor-sailed north and west of Inishturk and made for Achill Head in thick fog, which necessitated the use of the GPS navigator. My faith in the instrument was increasing. After Achill Head we rounded on to a north-east course for Blacksod Bay, which was cradled by the Mullet peninsula. Four miles north of Blacksod Point Lighthouse we dropped anchor in a small bay named Elly Bay, which was bordered by a sandy beach to the west. An isthmus of a third of a mile wide by a half-mile long separated the beach from the Atlantic on the western side of the peninsula. We had sailed into the eastern side of the bottom corner of the back of beyond. It was deathly quiet and peaceful and I was reminded of a line from the TV series *M*A*S*H*, uttered by the main character, Hawkeye: 'The book of the month club will never find me here.' I note from the logbook that there was the smell of fresh-mown grass and burning turf.

After dining on board we rowed ashore to seek out civilisation. We walked northwards for miles and saw nothing that resembled a pub. After turning back we came across two friendly ladies who showed us the only drinking hole in the area. We had passed it earlier and took no notice as it looked like a garage or similar workshop. We entered and found it empty. It was still bright and early for pubbing, we supposed, and the friendly girl, Kathleen, behind the bar assured us that the place would be busy later and so it was. We ordered two brandies with port – this was becoming our first drink of choice on making a landfall. After an hour the place started filling up and we found ourselves in the middle of a stag party for Paddy (believe it or not) who was getting married two days hence. Liam and I were treated like a novelty, being so far from home and all that. In the midst of the merriment that prevailed I advised the groom not to go through with the wedding before seeing the film, *Fatal Attraction*. We were invited to the afters of the wedding should we still be in the area, an offer we might have been enthusiastic about save for the fact that between us we didn't have one item of clothing that wasn't wrinkled. At the end of the night Kathleen drove us to our dinghy and on the way we had a discussion about the hype surrounding the upcoming millennium celebrations. The logbook for that day concludes: 'A pleasant night indeed'.

The next morning we headed south out of Blacksod Bay and rounded the headland and its two outlying islands: Duvillaun Mór and Duvillaun Beag, respectively Big Black Island and Small Black Island. After rounding we had a favourable westerly wind, which moved us along at six knots. We had Broad Haven in mind for our next stop but along the way we decided to avail of the favourable wind and keep sailing overnight and make landfall in Killybegs the following morning. At six in the evening we were off Erris Head and the long haul north eastward across Donegal Bay, covering 60 nautical miles, lay before us. At five in the morning we dropped anchor off Gallagher Bros fish plant in Killybegs Harbour and hit the bunks a considerable wallop. At half ten we were having breakfast in the Bay View Hotel after showering in the leisure centre. We came upon Aidean O'Connell, editor of *The Marine Times*, who kindly showed us a reliable mooring we could use during our stay. We duly took him up on the offer and came ashore again where a friend from college, Dominic Deeney, met us and played host to us during our time on land. Dominic drove us to his home in Dunkineely, where he and his wife Mary wined and dined us in true Donegal fashion. We stayed overnight in their home and the next day Dominic helped us provision the boat with groceries and fuel. At midday we were back on board *Eibhlís*. When I put the engine in gear after weighing anchor, the propeller snagged a mooring which had drifted under our stern in the calm waters of the harbour from an adjacent boat. We were truly propped and there was nothing for it only to get into my trunks, grab a knife between my teeth and jump over the side to cut away the line – but I didn't do that. A work boat from Sinbad Marine was doing a job in the harbour and I hailed them. A diver was subsequently sent down and he freed us from the errant mooring. Bill, who did the job for a reasonable fee, was very helpful and we gave him a bottle of wine for himself. We eventually got away from the harbour and into the bay to meet a slack westerly wind. We motored to Rathlin O'Birne Island under a scorching sun and soon after, the wind had gone and a long drawn-out swell of flat water bore us northwards. I made a corner cockpit seat from a piece of plywood I had obtained from Dominic and inscribed his name on it and the coordinates of the position where it was installed.

At around five in the morning around Bloody Foreland, a thick fog closed in and blotted out the dawn and the mainland to starboard. Tory Island to the north was lost to us too. The fog stayed with us all the way to our destination, which was Portsalon in Lough Swilly. I was navigating with the handheld GPS in the cockpit as we motored along the northern coast. Occasionally I would call out an instruction to Liam who was helming the boat and between us we blasted the fog horn at intervals. Our task was to change course to 115° true after Fanad Head to bring us down into the lough. As we approached we could see the form of the headland to our right about a mile off. My faith in electronic navigation took a giant leap. We made our way slowly south along the western coast of the lough and fifty minutes after Fanad, we picked up a visitor's mooring in Portsalon Harbour. After a brief look around at the spectacular harbour, we retired to our bunks. That evening Liam cooked spaghetti bolognaise and we stuffed ourselves under a clear sky and warm sunshine. A nice Merlot complemented the delicious meal.

Walking along the long almost empty beach later we remarked on the unspoilt beauty of the place, apart from the odd holiday home sticking out from the rich greenery. The sand was clean and golden on the beach which extended in an arc for about three miles. The beach has since been designated the second most beautiful beach in the world by *The Observer*.

The whole scene was reminiscent of an undiscovered paradise. We had one of the finest beaches I had ever seen to ourselves. The remoteness of the location no doubt explained the lack of tourists in the area. Later in the hostelry by the quayside we met a couple from Port Stewart who were very helpful regarding the next leg of our journey. They recommended Ballycastle in Antrim, where a new marina had just been completed.

At 0530 the next morning we made a course north-eastwards out of Lough Swilly with the landmark of Malin Head, our northernmost point, about three hours away. When the rounding came Liam and I marked the event by clinking mugs and consuming the leftovers of the previous day's meal. We then set on a course of 22° south of east which would bring us to Rathlin Sound and onto the entrance to Ballycastle. Roughly halfway across to Rathlin, we passed Inishowen Head and the entrance to Lough Foyle in the vicinity of which we were entering Northern Ireland waters. When voyaging in a boat, to put it simply, you fly your own country's ensign aft on your vessel and when entering a different territorial jurisdiction you fly a (small-sized) courtesy flag of the territory you are visiting. I asked Liam to haul up the UK flag, which he did after much cajoling and the threat of being put in irons by his captain.

In the late afternoon, we tied up at the new marina in Ballycastle and were immediately welcomed by independent councillor Chris McCaughan. He informed us that we were the first boat from the south in the marina. Chris took us under his wing while we were there, advising us where to eat and get a good pint, get rations, fuel and chandlery, etc. Before we departed, the councillor came on board and spent an hour talking politics, which naturally touched on the then relationship between north and south. He was an amiable fellow and eager that we depart with a favourable impression of Ballycastle. He need not have tried too hard because during our visit Liam and I had a very pleasant and relaxing time. Ballycastle is famous for its Old Lammas Fair, held on the last Monday and Tuesday in August each year. It is a celebration of the wheat harvest. Lammas (from an old English word meaning 'loaf mass') is primarily associated with Lammastide, an event in the ecclesiastical calendar that occurs around 1 August each year. John Henry MacAuley, a local shopkeeper, wrote a famous ballad about the fair but died in 1937 before his song became famous.

Liam spent one day on a trip to Campbeltown in Scotland which was about a 35-mile ferry trip from Ballycastle. I stayed behind and found plenty to do around the boat in preparation for the next leg of the voyage. We were approximately halfway round on our circumnavigation and pleased with our progress. As I was writing postcards on the deck of *Eibhlís* under pleasant sunshine, a small fishing boat pulled alongside with a crew of father (Nick) and son working out of Scotland and they gave me a basket of crab claws. We chatted for a while and talked of fishing and other stuff. They were impressed with *Eibhlís* and I filled them in on her history. When Liam returned we headed for the Harbour Bar and had a few scoops in the company of Brian and Chris who befriended us. There was an easy-going atmosphere in the pub and again we felt we were a novelty due to our being from the extremities of a south-west diagonal from where we stood. When time was called at the end of the night we were treated as if we were locals, if you get my drift.

The timing of our departure on the following day was crucial as we would be sailing through the narrow gap between north-eastern Ireland and Scotland, where a tidal stream of up to five knots can run and we wanted to be running with the stream. We sailed out of Ballycastle humming the air of 'The Auld Lammas Fair' with the intention of sailing overnight to Clogherhead. We had a fair wind and pleasant sunshine as far as Cushendall and overnight the wind slacked off and picked up strong from the south in the early morning. After passing Strangford Lough our headway was decreased by the stiff wind which was building up a fair chop in the sea. After a time we decided to make for Kilkeel in County Down. It was 13 July, the day after the parades and celebrations by Orangemen marking the victory of William of Orange over Catholic King James II at the Battle of the Boyne. As we sailed into the large fishing harbour of Kilkeel, which has a strong Unionist heritage, all the boats were bedecked with bunting and flags with red hands emblazoned on them for the previous day's event. It was a daunting feeling for us as we entered with our small Irish tricolour flying aft on our boat.

We finally settled on a berth outside a fishing boat and chatted with the only other two people visible on the pier. Surprisingly, one of them was a net merchant who knew several Dingle fishermen and knew one in particular, of whom he spoke well, who, I'm sure, would hold completely opposite views on the conflict between Catholics and Protestants – the ice was broken. We went to the Pier House for breakfast and shopped in an adjacent chandlery. Later we decided to stay put for the night on board *Eibhlís* and not explore the town. I cannot recall the exact reasons for the decision but the overpowering message displayed by the billowing cloth on the surrounding boats probably had a bearing on it.

The next day we passed Carlingford Lough a couple of miles down the coast and if we had gone in there rather than Kilkeel, *Eibhlís* would have been in all of Ireland's fjords over the course of my ownership of the vessel. Howth was our next stop. The wind had gone to the west, north-west force five to six and we found ourselves having the best sail of the cruise thus far. We zipped down the Irish Sea on glistening water with salt spray stinging our cheeks under the warm sunshine. The wind held steady all the way and after less than seven hours we tied up to a mooring in the harbour of Howth. We ate in the Bloody Stream ashore, had a few beers and made the obligatory phone calls. Liam had to keep constant contact with the lady who was running the bar for him at home while he enjoyed the life of a mariner. Liam also took a break from the galley that evening and we had Chinese takeaway on the boat, accompanied by a nice Bordeaux. When eating on the boat in harbour it is not a case of eating off our laps: the table is set with tablecloth, napkins and all the other accoutrements that go with civilised dining ashore.

We picked up provisions ashore the next morning along with a new crewman, Louis O'Coileán, who was joining the cruise for a couple of days. Around midday we departed from Howth for Arklow with a west, south-west wind gusting to force six at times. On the way down through the Irish Sea, Liam and I had remarked on how the eastern coast of Ireland was bland and lacking in the rugged and scenic beauty of the Atlantic side. This was evident too on the stretch we were on. The millennia of battering from storms had carved a spectacular profile on the western and southern coasts which in turn provided many sheltered coves amid the crags and cliffs. A map of Ireland is telling in the evidence of erosion on the west and the relatively benign influence the sea has had on the eastern coast.

We sailed as far as Wicklow Head and there we took down the foresail as the wind had come too close. Under engine and mainsail we took on the Arklow bank and I was amazed at the turbulent seas we encountered. This is a feature of shallows where wind-driven waves build up as they meet a bank. *Eibhlís's* six and a half tons was lifted and thrown from wave to wave in the agitated water, which had no discernible pattern and defied the wishes of the helmsman to find a clear path through the churning crests. The conditions were not conducive to cooking in the galley and Liam tried valiantly to keep the kettle bedded down on the stove and make sandwiches at the same time. In the cabin, anything that was not tied down or stowed away properly clattered around the cabin sole. It was the kind of motion that would give those prone to seasickness a hell of a time. After an hour of these exasperating conditions we were within sight of the entrance to Arklow. On entering the harbour we found a berth at the marina where *Eibhlís* was to have a longer stay than I had counted on.

Strong southerly winds were forecast for a number of days while *Eibhlís* was in Arklow and Liam reluctantly made a decision to go home overland. Louis had to make a similar call so I was left crewless. I was sorry to see them leave, especially Liam as he would have loved to complete the circumnavigation. I did what I would do often in the future when bad weather prevented the continuation of a cruise; I stayed with the boat. The knowledge is embedded in my subconscious before I set out on a cruise that I may be left without crew at some stage and when that happens I am grateful that the reason is weather-related and not due to disharmonious conditions on board the boat. So I knuckled down to wait and checked my address book to see how many friends I had left. When stranded far from home, I am reluctant to phone people and ask for help with bringing the boat home because by the time they arrive the weather may have changed for the worse again and they would either have to hang around waiting or head back home the way they came. I find it extremely unsettling when people are hanging around waiting on my say-so for something to happen, like heading out to sea, and there would be one occasion in the future where I would succumb to such underlying pressure and head out to sea only to turn back again.

I went on a day trip to Gorey in Wexford where Barry (the illustrator for this work) and I spent two years in college on a teacher-training course. It was there we engaged in our first collaboration: the cover of the Christmas college magazine for which Barry did the artwork and I the accompanying text. I also took in Wexford town and explored the harbour in case I might need to call in there when *Eibhlís* was under way again. It is a habitual thing with me, and probably many other sailors, that when I am in a harbour town while travelling overland I check out the layout of the harbour, its entrance and facilities for future reference. I checked out every vessel in the Arklow marina and along the pier and came across the *Ros Dubh*, a former Dingle fishing boat from which I often got a strap of fish in my younger days. It was also festival time in the town and there was a good Chinese restaurant where I dined occasionally. A few good pubs with a range of entertainments took care of some of my evenings. I got the boat ready to go the minute the weather permitted. I had resigned myself to sailing the boat onward towards home on my own.

After five days, the wind went to the west and moderated. I left the harbour at eight in the morning. When I got out into the Irish Sea, I found that I was not prepared. As I hauled up the mainsail I discovered that the turn button at the foot of the sail track, which held the sail hanks captive, had come loose resulting in the luff of the sail flying loose in the wind. I thought, 'Liam, why have you abandoned me?' It took me twenty minutes in a rolling sea to re-house the hanks again and get underway. I pointed *Eibhlís* due south, lashed the tiller and boiled two duck eggs I had purchased at a street market the day before.

I had a steady and fair wind for about four hours. A bird I couldn't identify, as my naturalist (Liam) was back in Dingle pulling pints, perched on the foredeck and stayed with me for some time. In the vicinity of Rosslare there was ferry activity and soon after I sailed between Tuscar Rock and the mainland. The coastline was getting interesting again. The south-east corner of the country marks the change from ordinary to extraordinary. After leaving Tuscar behind I headed for the Saltee Islands, which were due south of the entrance to Kilmore Quay, my destination. When entering the harbour in Kilmore there are two wide walls, one to port and one to starboard, which 'blind off' the actual harbour. It is a bit disconcerting as one never knows what to expect when one enters. A bit of caution is needed and positioning is paramount as another vessel may be on the way out as you enter. It is vital to hug the northern wall when going in and the southern one coming out.

After tying up at the marina I visited the village, which was then largely a fishing community. The marina was relatively new. A decommissioned lightship, *Guillemot*, is imposing and buried into the concrete beside the marina car park. It is now a maritime museum. As I approached the centre of the village I noticed that traditional thatched houses were common. I found that the village got its name from the Irish, Cé na Cille Móire, 'quay of the big church'. It was evident that the village was veering into the tourism market with the addition of the marina from where sea angling boats for hire appeared to be a popular thing. The facilities ashore for the visiting yachtsman were meagre. A small chandlery would not go astray.

Lightship Guillemot in Kilmore Quay

At ten the next morning in slack winds I departed from Kilmore Quay and motor-sailed along the southern coast. I had no particular destination in mind. My aim was to make headway to the west and decide later in the day where I would pull in for the night. Sailing alone is different. I had done it often before and in the future I would spend many hours on my own at sea, sometimes out of necessity, as on this leg. A boat of *Eibhlís*'s size is manageable for the solo sailor, though I try not to be out there on my own when the sea is challenging. I feel that if I was to rely on crew to take the boat out, on short trips especially, my boat would end up tied to the marina most of the time. When going on an extended cruise I normally have crew lined up. Sailing in good company is a whole different thing from being out there on your own, though there are times when being at one with the elements has a particular, perhaps selfish, attraction. As I made my way west I was looking forward to getting to Union Hall as I had made arrangements before leaving Kilmore to pick up Louis again and a few other friends to continue to Dingle with me. With that coming up, I didn't mind spending a few more days on my own.

After eleven hours sailing I dropped anchor off Youghal town and cooked a meal which, once consumed, knocked me out completely. I stayed put for the night at anchor. Early next morning I was ferried ashore by a kind gent named Sammy. I picked up diesel, water and food and was ferried back to *Eibhlís*. Managing the transfer of stores in my rubber dinghy would have been laborious as I was anchored a good bit off the slipway. Sammy was a godsend to the operation. At ten thirty I got underway on a flat sea. It would be another day of motor-sailing.

After Knockadoon Head south of Youghal, I followed a course for the Old Head of Kinsale; thereafter Seven Heads appeared and as night fell the familiar Galley Head Lighthouse was blinking when I was abeam to it. In darkness I entered Union Hall harbour and tied up outside the fishing vessel *Oileán Glas*. There was only one thing to do after spending so much time alone. It was Saturday night so I made haste to Moloney's bar for a bit of banter with Johnny and the locals and a very welcome jar. I met up with Johnny Donovan, another former shipwright student. Johnny and I always make contact when I am in the area. We had a few and filled in the news gaps since we last met. Johnny has a keen interest in Gaelic football and is always anxious to hear about Kerry's prospects in the run-up to the All-Ireland. I bluff it as much as I can with him as my interest and enthusiasm falls well short of his, but he knows that too. My brother Michael, who is a huge follower of the game, and Johnny have a right old natter about the sport when they meet and if Johnny Moloney's uncle James is in the pub, a good exchange is guaranteed.

Before the night ended, Johnny Moloney (Johnnies abound) produced a pot of cooked crab claws on top of the counter and there was a furious clattering of heavy spoons and pieces of meat flying in the air for most of an hour – all the better to make us thirsty for a few more beers. You can't beat those cute west Cork barmen.

After a break of three days, which I welcomed, I was joined by Louis again. Paul Mitchell, an acquaintance from Castleisland, and his friends Nick LeDouc and Martin Roe completed the new crew. We sailed out of Union Hall on a warm day with a fair wind bound for Oileán Chléire. It was good to be underway again after the couple of days ashore. Johnny Moloney, whose hospitality is always genuine, likes to keep you as long as possible in his embrace. Paul's friends Nick and Martin, who were first-timers to *Eibhlís*, were savouring the spectacle of the southern Irish coast. There was a good atmosphere amongst the crew and anticipation for a good voyage prevailed – and that was the way things turned out. In looking back, *Eibhlís* had a fitting last leg to her circumnavigation.

The Stags rocks off Toe Head looked menacing. In 1986, the *Kowloon Bridge* lost steerage and sank on the southern end of these dangers. For twenty-six years the shipwreck held the record for being the largest in Europe, but in 2012 that was surpassed by the *Costa Concordia* disaster. When we had the Kedge, an island east of Baltimore that looks like a huge loaf of bread, behind us we headed for the Gascanane Sound on the north-eastern corner of Oileán Chléire. We passed north of Oileán na nEán and worked our way along the island to its north harbour. At eight thirty that evening we tied up outside the ferry in Oileán Chléire, had a cook-up on board and retired to Club Chléire where we enjoyed a convivial few hours amongst the good people of the island. A song may have been sung.

The next morning the engine would not start and Louis and Paul spent an hour looking for the fault. They eventually found that it was an electrical problem. An oil-sodden electrical terminal with black insulation tape around its end had stopped making contact with the engine. While effecting the repair, Paul, who was good with this stuff, would look at Louis and then at me in wonderment. It was clear that I was being admonished for going to sea with such a shoddy set-up. Paul was right, of course. In those days I was a bit flippant about my engine. I had it in my head that once I had sail power, I would be able to get out of most tricky situations should the engine fail. Paul will be delighted to find that my thinking has changed in that regard.

Just before midday we got under way. The day was extremely hot and the wind blew force four from the south. It was an ideal sailing day. After passing Mizen Head we knuckled down to the long haul to Dursey. Food was prepared by Nick, who was proving to be a good hand all round. He had fallen in love with the boat right away. At Dursey Island we decided to go through the sound, which is always an interesting experience, and on exiting we hoisted a spinnaker, which took us all the way to Puffin Island. From there we goose-winged the jib and that carried us to Bray Head. On entering Dingle Bay there was a great feeling of coming home after the circumnavigation that began thirty-one days previous. We were close-hauled from Bray Head to the entrance to Knightstown on Valentia Island. It had been a fantastic sailing day. At 2230 we tied up to a visitor's buoy off the pier at Knightstown and visited Boston's Bar and the Royal Hotel for refreshments and, as a good friend of mine would say, for a thorough debriefing of the day's events.

The final leg of *Eibhlís*'s round-Ireland voyage began at noon the following day, a day that presented us with sunshine and a brisk westerly wind, which instilled the want for further adventure. After passing Valentia Lighthouse a course was set for the Blasket Islands and *Eibhlís*, on a beam reach, chewed up the distance between Valentia and the Blasket Sound. We dropped anchor off the beach of An Blascaod Mór. Louis and I stayed on board and the three explorers, Paul, Nick and Martin, rowed ashore to the sandy beach in the dinghy. Two hours later, with all crew accounted for, we weighed anchor and made east for Dingle Harbour. The sail east along the coast was thrilling; the wind had freshened and gone to the north-west. We were heeled over with the starboard gunnel awash as the wind blew off the land. When we were abeam of Ventry Harbour, *Eibhlís* was on her ear and everyone on board was clambering for the high side of the vessel. All the way to the entrance of Dingle Harbour, *Eibhlís* maintained her dogged course as if she was aware of the need to put on a show on her return to her home port.

At 1900 hours we tied up at Dingle Marina and had a good meal in Coco and Pol's café. Later the crew and various roadies, who were following our adventures, retired to the Skellig Hotel for a night of celebration and general merriment to mark the completion of the voyage, which concluded in my logbook with the words: '*DG, Deo Gratias*'.

Chapter 6

Union Hall and Wally's Dinghy

'How are ye all west along?' That was Wally's salute the first time I met him. I had arrived in Union Hall with three crewmen. We were on our way to Brittany from Dingle and it was a given that we would spend a night in the west Cork village before setting sail south for the Scilly Isles off Land's End, which would act as a stopover before the final leg of the journey to the north coast of France. I had been calling to Union Hall regularly prior to that in the summertime and had become aware of Wally and he of me. It was a natural development that we should eventually connect and have words since we were both men of the sea and had that commonality which draws seafaring folk together.

Wally was a large-framed man who gave the impression that he was awkward in the field of manoeuvrability but he always seemed to get by. A stiffness of gait didn't seem to inhibit the end result of his mechanical motions in any way. He could be described as never being in a hurry or as someone who possessed an acute awareness of the maxim that when God made time, He made lots of it. In his sixties, he had jet black hair and the skin on his square-jawed face was smooth and tanned all year round. No doubt he possessed genes from long-forgotten ancestors who hailed from Andalusia or farther afield. He spoke with a mix of a west Cork, musical accent and an imported twang of indiscernible origin. His attire was invariably a fisherman's jumper with shirt collar protruding and dark-coloured slacks, which in part concealed the wideness of his girth.

Wally was mostly interested in serious conversation relating to matters on land and sea. He could talk authoritatively about local events and give a knowledgeable account of the historic lay of the land. He knew several fishermen from 'west along', including some from the fishing town of Dingle. We both discovered that we had common acquaintances on the periphery of Dingle Bay. But Wally also liked a bit of 'gaff'. His humour was mostly matter-of-fact and he was often hilarious unbeknownst to himself. I could tell him a tall tale and have him enthralled most of the way until he'd say, 'By God, O'Connor, you must think I'm an awful fool. Ye Kerry fellas think we are a right bunch of "luadramáns" down here.'

We had many a good chat and playful banter over a pint in J. Moloney's pub. That was in the day when people went to the pub to socialise and meet friends in a convivial atmosphere. The pub was three doors up the street from Wally's and was the centre of the social life of the village. Inside the door to the right was Wally's berth. There he commanded his corner and was in a position to oversee the general comings and goings of the place.

Wally had a boat, a twenty-six-foot half decker with a scant wheelhouse fitted aft of the deck on the starboard side, which he used for some small-time fishing around the coves and inlets of Glandore Bay. The boat's engine had a distinctive sound, like the one from *The African Queen*: the chug-chunk, chug-chunk announced its coming long before it became visible to anyone expecting its landfall at Union Hall Pier. Its commander could then be seen standing to the side outside the wheelhouse with his long arm extended inside to manipulate the wheel. During one of his excursions around the bay, Wally acquired an orange-coloured rubber dinghy which was washed up on the shore. I subsequently saw this in the backyard of Wally's house when once invited to partake of tea, which was duly poured from a wide-based aluminium teapot that would have been an ideal example for explaining the inverted cone frustum in one of my geometry classes. It happened that I was in the market for a tender for my own boat at the time and the orange dinghy fitted the bill perfectly. I broached the subject with its newfound owner over a drink and he suggested that I call to the house on Sunday for dinner and that we would strike a bargain in an atmosphere of dining and relaxed companionship. In other words it was to be a working lunch on his home turf.

On a fine sunny day in late July I arrived in Wally's kitchen, which was to the front of the house and looked out onto the main street of the village. The dining table was directly inside the front window. I sat facing the window and my host fitted into a well-worn chair in the left corner that backed onto a painted kitchen dresser. The stove was to the left of that. On the table a plate was heaped with boiled potatoes with their skins cracking smiles and revealing white furry insides. The bacon and cabbage was on our plates, already served from a pot on the stove onto large plates. A red and yellow floral pattern circled the food. A jug of milk and two sturdy mugs were placed strategically and Kerry Gold butter in its foil wrapper, with an ivory-handled knife piercing it at an angle of forty-five degrees, stood at the ready. A bottle of YR brown sauce completed what was on offer.

We dug into the meal and chatted amicably like long-time friends do. People were passing the window, throwing shadows across the table, which prompted Wally to remark: 'By God, there's a lot of traffic out there today.' I imagined that my bachelor host often sat in the corner chair as he dined alone while passers-by intermittently broke the solitude of his day. Though he never seemed lonely. If anything, he came across as having great independence and confidence. I got the impression that he valued good company and the exchange of ideas and stories.

'I suppose one hundred, maybe one twenty, would be a fair price for the dinghy, Wally,' I ventured as we were into the meal proper.

'Eat up there awhile, John.'

The food was good Sunday fare. I could have done without the milk though. The buttered spuds were pure heaven.

'What will you let it go for Wally? And remember we are old friends.'

'I suppose it's worth two hundred and fifty easy, John, and eat up them fine potatoes. You need a bit of fattening, you know.'

'I didn't expect that you'd be asking that much, seeing as you kind of found it. What about one forty?'

''Tis hard to beat a good plate of bacon and cabbage – and good company while you're eating it. What do you think, John?'

Wally lopped more potatoes onto my plate and reached to the pot on the hob with a long ladle to scoop up more cabbage for the two of us. We munched for another while, each waiting for the next instalment of the bargaining process.

'I'd probably go as far as one sixty just because it's you, Wally, and especially seeing that you invited me round for this wonderful dinner.'

'You're a wily one alright, O'Connor. There's no cobwebs in ye lads from west along.'

And so it went on. Whenever I made a lowly offer, Wally countered with quips about the quality of the meal and the effort it took to bring it to table. We had an enjoyable thrust and parry and finally agreed on a price, which was sealed over two mugs of tea so strong they would put a wrinkle on a pig's back.

A few years later Wally became scarce around the place. I'd been told he wasn't well. Then one year I found that he had died since my previous visit. I visited the graveyard on a sparkling summer's day and was hit with the realisation that I never knew his surname. In fact I didn't know his Christian name either. It was an incredibly stupid dilemma to be in: not knowing the name, or date of passing, of the one you had come to seek out. I lingered awhile and looked to the sea from the elevated place of rest. A yacht was heeled over by the brisk southerly wind and a fishing boat was heading for home, ushered in by a cloud of seagulls. A groundsman carrying a scythe entered and began to cut the high grass between the graves. I explained my predicament and he guided me to Wally's last port of call. I thought that he would approve of the location; above the sea with the cry of the gulls and even the distant sound of a boat engine chugging along the coast. I said my farewell to Wally and as I made to go the man tending the graves said: 'Ye were friends, you and Wally?' 'Yes,' I said, 'Wally and I were friends.'

***

While the American president has Camp David and the Pope has Castel Gondolfo to retreat to, I have Union Hall. Since I sailed there in 1987, I have returned every summer bar two. My association with the west Cork fishing village stems from the fact that I have several past shipwright students from the area and they always make me feel welcome, among them John and Finbar Moloney. On voyages south to Cornwall and Brittany I have used the harbour as a staging stopover before the long haul to the Isles of Scilly and beyond. During the biannual Glandore Classic Boat Regatta I would drop anchor there or tie up to a mooring in the harbour, which I put down in later years with help from the Moloney brothers.

On one of my earlier visits, when we were staying over, my crew and I walked up the village after arriving and went into Moloney's pub to see if we could borrow a car from Johnny to go to Glandore, where showers were available to yachtsmen attending the Regatta. Paul, a cousin of Johnny's, was seated at the counter and put his keys on the counter and said we could take his car away. My companions were astounded at the generosity of this man, who didn't know us at all then. This was a fine example of the welcoming spirit that one encounters in the village.

Through my former (shipwright) students, I got to know many of their extended families. Donovans, Moloneys, Deaseys and McCarthys are but some of the families whose doors were open to me while I holidayed in their midst. Then there were the friends who were thrust upon me by virtue of knowing Johnny Moloney and frequenting his hostelry. Nick Mosley, Eddie Bird and Diarmuid Dineen were always sure to show up and give of their own brand of hospitality.

Eddie and his wife Kath alternate between living in London and their summer home in Union Hall, 'Tig na nÉan', high up on a hill with a spectacular panorama of the sea to the south. They love to entertain. Several of my crews and I have availed of their generosity in the elevated haven with its view of the Stag Rocks in the distance. The couple take great joy in having people visit. I have on several occasions been a welcome guest in their home, whether for morning coffee and scones or a multicourse evening meal of fish, meat and pudding, with interesting Bordeaux and robust Zinfandels being served in between. The invited guests are always at ease in the lofty heights overlooking the Celtic Sea. At a barbecue on a clear night with the stars sprinkled over head and the odd cloud calling for a look, there is a sense of being apart from the world below and a feeling, later, of going 'back down' at the end of the night.

A tailor by trade, now retired, Eddie is precise in all that he does. His historic, exacting need for precision while in the rag trade now flows over into his daily life. This I understand as I, too, have a similar background in measurement. During the construction of a semi-conical roof for a recently added solarium (to his house), a pattern for a diminishing slate for each course of the structure was prepared by the former tailor. The polygonal substructure of box steel was also marked out with dimensions and angles to the nearest millimetre. He was a constant source of tormenting exactitude to the local carpenters (J. Moloney included) who were doing the job. But that was Eddie's way and the interaction with the builders alluded to above took place in an atmosphere of light-heartedness and good will. Eddie knew full well that the men employed were competent and could do the work. When I was first shown the finished product, I was naturally asked by Eddie, in the company of my former students, for a critical appraisal and that of course led to a whole new pile of banter and efforts at one-upmanship by all in the room. At a later time,

Eddie was concerned about a whistling sound caused by the wind, which emanated from underneath the double doors to the conservatory. After a discussion about the fit of the door and the natural movement of timber, which probably gave rise to a gap of micro dimensions, he had me down on the ground listening to the whistle: 'Can you hear it, John? What do you think?' he inquired. I was of a mind to say it would fit in well with the Dingle Fife and Drum Band.

***

Diarmuid, a pilot by profession and a keen sailor, has also opened up his home to my summer entourages. He and I have journeyed on mini-cruises around West Cork. He is good company and always very obliging when I visit the area. The old house where he and his family reside, on the outskirts of Leap, was renovated by him with particular attention to the details of conservation and tradition. On his windows, he shunned double-glazing because the sectional timber dimensions required for the stiles and bars would be contrary to the originals. It is hard to keep up with the exactitude of some of those west Cork fellows. Diarmuid can be fun too and, like a lot of his cronies from those parts, he doesn't mind getting one over on a Kerry fellow from time to time – in a well-meaning sort of way. There is an unofficial twinning of the two ports, Dingle and Union Hall, between our mutual circle of friends, which also extends to the off-season. The west Cork crowd visit my hometown a few times a year to see, among other things, if we are getting ahead of them in any way.

Whenever I dock in Union Hall, the word seems to get about before I finish the trek from the pier to the village. I hear remarks like, 'I heard you were in', or, 'I saw you tying up below'. Often, on the way east along the coast from Cape, I pass some of the local boats, the Moloney's *Charlotte* included, and we make contact on the VHF. A bucket of crab claws or a lobster is often dropped onto my deck soon after mooring.

In January 2012, the small community found itself in the glare of the world media following the sinking of the fishing boat *Tit Bonhomme* at the harbour's entrance with the loss of five souls. The people rallied immediately and put normal life in the village on hold for most of a week to help with the rescue and recovery effort. Their response was hailed nationally and representative members were later awarded for their exceptional efforts. A memorial garden to the souls lost at sea in Union Hall and its vicinity was unveiled in the summer of 2012.

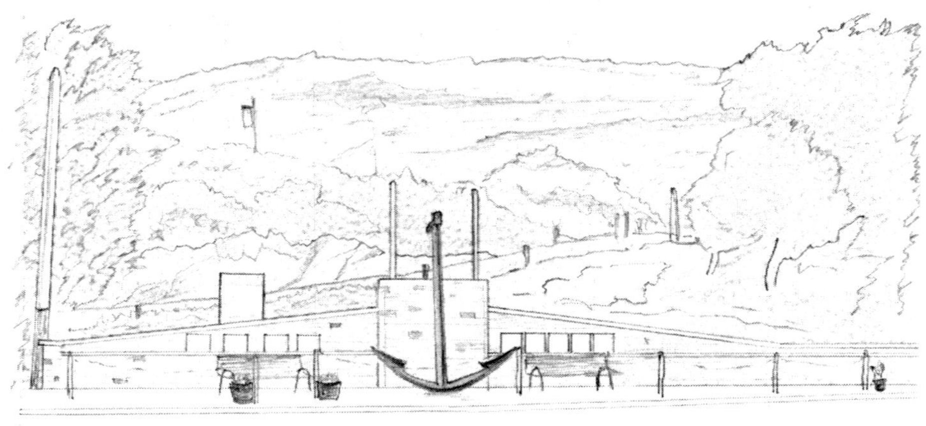

Union Hall memorial garden

West Cork has one of the most popular and beautiful sections of coastline on the whole of our island. It has small coves and larger harbours, which are conveniently arrayed for day-sailing or more extensive voyaging. It is possible to have breakfast, lunch and dinner in separate locations and enjoy comfortable sailing in between. While the coast from Dingle south, as a whole, offers several inviting stopovers, it is after passing the Mizen that a menu of close-proximity anchorages opens up to the cruising sailor.

Chapter 7

Guernsey, St Malo and Dinan

In the year 2000, I would cover new ground with *Eibhlís* and before that summer was over *Eibhlís* would have clocked up more than 4,000 nautical miles since I picked her up in Hamble in 1996. Both my regular crew at the time and I had a desire for travel and adventure in those days. The boat was proving to be a very comfortable and reliable sailing-cruising boat and obviously we enjoyed cruising together. Mark came to the boat with a broad knowledge of sailing and navigation and Liam had experience at sea and a good grasp of seamanship. Our fourth crewman that year was Gerald O'Driscoll, who had sailed with me on *Polyanna* in 1993 and he brought his own gifts to the table. On this trip he also brought along his trumpet and I packed my guitar. There was a foundation for a good voyage – but it had its glitches and there are still lashes owing according to the end pages of the logbook where notes of infractions were recorded.

Again Nicholas crewed with us (Mark, Liam and I) to west Cork and this time his place was taken by Gerald – Nick and a friend Joe were meeting up with friends in Oileán Chléire. In Cape we picked up Gerald, who was doing a gig there for the night with a jazz band. We sailed south to our usual layover, St Mary's. The sail south was pleasant. When we were about 20 miles south from Ireland we came across a pod of pilot whales. Later on, a pigeon landed on the deck and stayed with us for over ten hours through the night and flew away to the east in the morning.

Another heartbeat onboard

Gerald was interested in navigating with the GPS and he plotted our course at various intervals and marked it on the chart. *Polyanna* did not have GPS installed when he last crewed with me. It was eleven at night when we got in to St Mary's and there was some confusion about the compass bearing on our approach to the harbour. Something similar to the suspected magnetic anomaly we experienced on *An tSiocháin* in 1983. We brought the boat around to the south harbour the next day and lay to our own anchor. This saved the fee for the visitors' moorings in the north harbour. There were grumblings the following morning from the crew, who had difficulty sleeping in the sea roll that the south harbour is noted for in certain conditions. I told them I had a perfect night's sleep. We stayed into the second day. Liam cooked lemon chicken with rice and got five stars from Gerald, who was a good hand at putting together a meal himself. Mark and I were being pampered. We showed Gerald the town and had a few beers.

At 0830 hours on 28 June, we set sail for Guernsey in the Channel Islands. The wind turned strong from the south-east after a time and we decided for Newlyn in Cornwall. On the way the sea was an amazing misty green and the sky a clear blue. 'All's well', the log entry reads in Mark's hand. We berthed alongside a fishing boat at the pier in Newlyn. There is never any problem doing that; the fishermen are largely accommodating in that regard. It was a new port for Gerald and he subsequently took in Penzance as well during our stay there. He was AWOL for quite a time.

We eventually got underway to Guernsey the next morning. At the start of the south-easterly trip, we were doing seven and a half knots with all sails hauled tight for the southerly wind. The distance to Guernsey from the Scillies is about 135 miles. When I am calculating the time it will take to get to a destination I divide the mileage by five, so for this voyage, assuming fair sailing conditions, it would take us twenty-seven hours to St Peter Port in Guernsey. *Eibhlís* averages five knots (nautical miles per hour) over a long journey. In exceptional situations, like being on a beam reach and driven by a stiff wind, she will do better than that.

Gerald and I shared the eight-to-twelve watch and reminisced about our history in the IT Tralee, among other things. He was keen to learn more about the workings of *Eibhlís* and was enjoying the overnight aspect of the trip. The night was clear and bright and the phosphorescence around the boat where she cut through the water was spectacular. Throughout that leg of the journey we came across dolphins that ushered us on our way like they were giving us a guard of honour. Gerald picked up a fine boathook from the water and, not to be outdone, Liam spotted a fairly new fender adrift, which was duly hauled on board. Both crew now had credits in the log book.

St Peter Port has a phenomenal tidal range. It can reach a staggering eight metres at times. When we arrived there at two in the afternoon we had to wait, tied up to a waiting berth, until the tide was right. The marinas, of which there are three with one for visitors, always have enough water for berthed yachts to float, but there is a sill at the entrance to the marinas over which a boat needs sufficient water to enter and exit, hence the waiting berth until the tide filled. The harbour has been well developed to cope with the rise and fall of the tides.

Guernsey is a bailiwick which has its own parliament and is run by a sheriff on behalf of the Crown, as is Jersey and Sark and a few others which make up the Channel group. The town of St Peter Port is a fair size and at the time was busy with the many tourists the islands get. The island is clean and orderly. One gets a feeling that it is a no-nonsense kind of place. We were stopped from setting up a barbeque on *Eibhlís's* stern, obviously a fire safety precaution. Gerald had spent time in Guernsey in the past, working in a boatyard, and was familiar with the run of the place. We met some of his friends on a night out, after which we retired to *Eibhlís* for a trumpet and guitar session, not knowing if that too was against the law.

Early on 2 July we departed for St Malo on the north coast of France. The voyage southwards was pleasant with great weather and a fair wind. When we crossed over the line into French territory, Gerald got out his trumpet and played the 'La Marseillaise' as Liam hoisted the courtesy flags, one with the black and white stripes of Brittany and the other with the colours of France.

Into French waters

We arrived in St Malo on the day France had won the European Football Championship and as soon as we hit town there was the inevitable jubilant atmosphere in the air. We were embraced as if we were their own and before long we were wearing the colours and trying to sing songs in French. It was pretty much like being in Kerry on All-Ireland day.

St Malo is a wonderful walled city with an old-fashioned feel to it. It has several cobbled streets with old and new shops, restaurants and café bars. There are many historical buildings, including a fine cathedral. The city swells with tourists in summertime and there are plenty of facilities for sailors. We stayed in St Malo for a day and a half. I would have liked to stay longer in the St Malo area but I had to accommodate my crew's wishes as well. Our next stop was about fourteen miles upriver from St Malo: a lovely old town called Dinan.

The Rance River, from St Malo to Dinan, was harnessed for the production of electricity in 1966 and created the world's first tidal power station and kept that record for forty-five years until the Sihwa Lake project in South Korea opened. The Rance Barrage is an extraordinary engineering achievement. The ebbing and flowing of the river drives twenty-four turbines, which produce a huge amount of electricity. There is a lock gate on the barrage that controls the through-flow of traffic. Yachts traversing the river need to know the times of opening of the lock. A timetable with the relevant opening times is available free from local marinas in the vicinity. When approaching the lock from either side, waiting buoys are provided for visiting yachts. These buoys can be tricky to pick up depending on the run and height of the tide when approaching them.

The Rance snakes its way up to Dinan which is a relatively small but very picturesque town. It is halved by the river, which has an old bridge joining the two sides. Yachts tie up at the wall on the starboard hand as they approach. The river bank is lined with shops and cafés and the setting is quaint on a fine day when the river is full. The town is much quieter than St Malo and has a homelier feel to it. It is popular with yachting people and overland tourists. We found a café bar, which was friendly and had a very accommodating barman who looked after our every need while we visited. We did some shopping for local wines the morning before we left and got a send-off from some of the locals.

Dinan, France

When navigating on a river like the Rance that has single buoys marking the channel, it is vital, on a falling tide especially, to hug the buoys on the correct side. On the way downriver from Dinan, the tide was falling and it was necessary to stay in the channel, which had sufficient water for *Eibhlís's* draught. Gerald was on the helm and I had imparted the procedure to him. About halfway down the river I was down below at the cooker and I felt the boat come to a sudden stop as it buried its keel into the muddy bottom of the riverbed. I thought to myself, 'Not Truro again'. I leapt to the cockpit and looked over the side. We were too far away from the starboard marker; it should have been right next to the hull but wasn't.

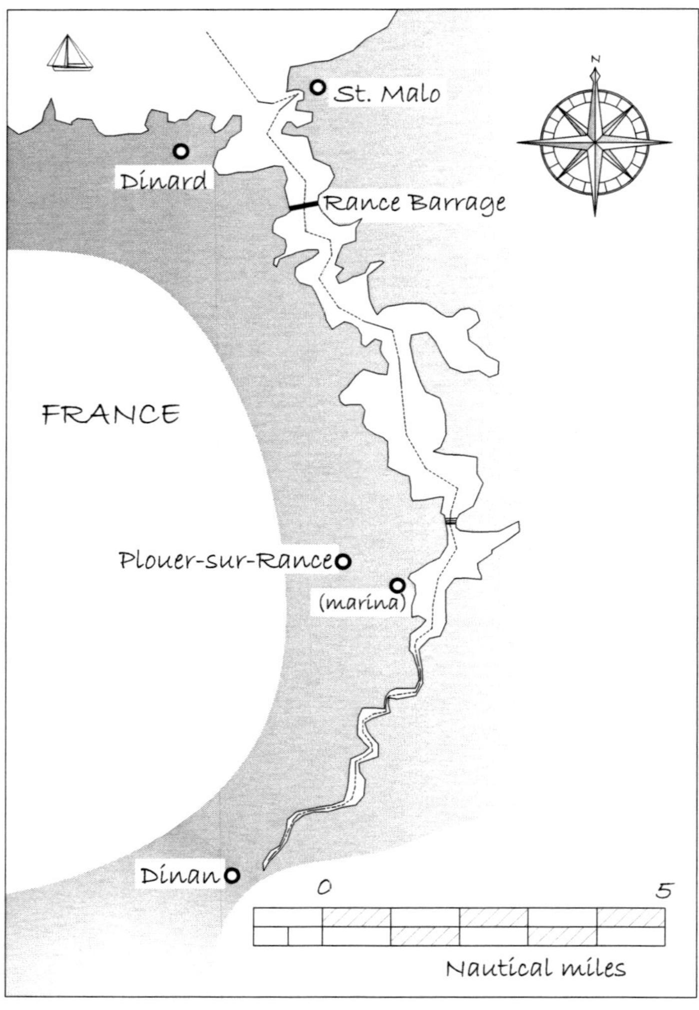

There is confusion among 'new' sailors about the handing of individual buoys in a river situation; when entering a port like Dinan, or indeed entering any port in Western Europe (region A) from the sea, the buoys on your right-hand side are green and you keep them to starboard; conversely, the red buoys are to port. But what a lot of novice sailors forget is that when leaving port, the reverse must be observed, i.e. greens on the left and reds on the right. I am not saying that confusion about the buoyage resulted in our grounding, but there are times when it can be disconcerting especially if you get sidetracked by a conversation going on beside you or are involved in an exchange of riddles or funny stories. Anyway the upshot of the error was that *Eibhlís* was aground, again. We struck at 1530 hours and didn't get afloat till 2200 hours.

Gerald was apologetic and concerned as to the ramifications of the mishap. I cheered him up when I told him of my own mishap in Truro River. The boat dried out and we were able to get off and walk on the riverbed. Photos were taken but thankfully I never got to see them. In those days you took rolls of photos and left them into the chemist shop for processing. A week later the photos were collected, you looked at them, put them in a drawer and never saw them again, unlike now where ... no, I won't start on that.

While *Eibhlís* was on her ear, it was impossible to find a comfortable corner to relax in due to the angle of the hull. A proper meal could not be prepared and going to the heads was definitely out. Gerald was cowering in the sail stowage area lest he got any dagger looks from his crew mates. The bilge water was making its way up the side of the hull around the starboard bunks. Personal belongings had to be tied up on the high side. The voyage was on a downer and quietness permeated throughout *Eibhlís*. It was inconvenient to say the least that we came upon our misfortune in an uninhabited part of the river. There were no café bars close by where we could wait out our predicament. We endured and watched the returning water make its way up along the side of the boat until we floated off and made our way downriver. It was getting dark and the barrage would not be opening till morning so we pulled into a small marina, Moulin de Plouer, upriver from the barrage and berthed alongside a yacht named – wait for it – *Stress Relief*.

In the morning we walked quite a distance to get diesel. It was not readily available in Dinan. The kind lady, Isabella, running the marina did not charge us for our overnight stay. She must have been told of our misfortune by one of the crew. We had breakfast on board before we left the marina and headed for the barrage where we had a short wait south of the lock before the road lifted and allowed us through. The weather was getting fresh; a force five wind from the north-east was blowing and squally showers had us all donning our wet gear. Our destination was home and through the night the conditions are described in the logbook as 'black, dirty and uncomfortable'.

At 1130 hours the next day we were 60 miles out from the Scillies and at four that evening I reefed the main sail as the wind was blowing force six and gusting from the north-west. At a quarter to eleven that night we tied *Eibhlís* to the pier in St Mary's and took a breather after what had turned out to be an exhausting trip. Liam cooked a meal while we were tied to the pier and we discussed the apparently worsening weather while we dined. After the meal we took the boat to a visitor's mooring in the north harbour. Even though it was blowing a bit I wanted the security of the mooring rather than my own anchor. We then stayed put for the night.

After getting a weather fax the following day at the harbour office, we saw that the weather didn't look good for the following days. Gerald decided to go home overland, not knowing how long we would be delayed in the island. Mark, Liam and I weathered it out, going ashore in the dinghy from time to time and passing the time as best we could. Every day we checked the mooring line for chaffing because the motion of the sea was putting it under pressure. We awoke one morning to see three yachts grounded on the beach at Hugh Town after their mooring warps gave way.

The inconvenience of being on board at a mooring in bad weather for a prolonged period prompted us to spend a couple of nights ashore. We booked into a B&B and spent time reading and talking about the weather, among other things, and how the situation we found ourselves in was a result of our grounding on the river Rance. It was mooted that if we hadn't gone aground on the way down river from Dinan, we would have been ahead of the bad weather and made it home to the south of Ireland ahead of the strong northerlies, which now prevailed. But of course that was nonsense. Who knows what obstructions would have been in our path had we proceeded according to plan? It is not prudent to try to second-guess nature and its designs. When the unexpected is laid before us we deal with it because it is really the natural course of events.

After our two nights ashore we got a window in the weather which we thought would enable us to sail north towards home. We stocked up on diesel and rations and readied the boat for the journey. At four in the morning on 12 July, we departed from St Mary's for home, which was any port in the south of Ireland. After sailing north against a strong north-west wind that was forecasted to strengthen during the day, I had reservations about continuing the (at least) thirty hour journey. We were not making any significant headway on the lumpy sea and I felt that we could be out there tacking at the whim of increasing wind strength for an indefinite period. In those days weather forecasting data was not as accessible as it is now. In retrospect I believe I set out because I knew that Liam and Mark were anxious to get home to their respective domestic and business commitments. I felt under pressure to get my crew home and it was not a comfortable or desirous call for me when I suggested to Liam and Mark when we were thirty-two miles out from St Mary's that I felt we should turn back. It was one of those decisions whereby you cannot gauge afterwards if it was necessary – I use that word deliberately because there was no right or wrong at issue.

On the way back to St Mary's we had a quick spin as the wind was with us. We were accompanied by a school of dolphins that stayed with us for more than an hour. At seven in the evening we were moored again off Hugh Town. We had a farewell meal ashore in Portchressa as Liam and Mark had decided to go home overland the next day. The weather was to remain unsettled for a number of days. We brought the boat to the pier next morning, where my two crewmen got on the *Scillonian* ferry to begin their journey home. I returned to the mooring with *Eibhlís* and after tying up I sat down and thought of my options. I was alone again with *Eibhlís*, but not for long.

On the following day I took the boat around to the south harbour and dropped anchor. The wind was still strong from the north but the sun was shining and when I sat on the sheltered beach at Portchressa later in the day, there was a Mediterranean feel to the place. I got some more weather faxes at the harbour office and was happy to see that high pressure was going to build over the area, as well as Ireland and England, in the coming days. After a walk around the now over-familiar environs of the harbour, I rowed back out to *Eibhlís* and found a few jobs to do, including filling in the logbook. I looked astern and saw a familiar sight: *Second Wind* was anchored astern of me. She must have come in as I was down below. The boat had been on a round-the-world voyage for two years and was returning home. I got into the dinghy and rowed over to greet the crew. Seamus O'Donoghue, his brother Colmán and their brother-in-law Kevin Ogden were on board. Seamus told me he had recognised *Eibhlís* on entering the harbour. We had a brief chat about their travels, which I'm sure would fill a considerable tome, and I filled them in on my own circumstances.

Eibhlís and Second Wind at anchor in St. Mary's, Isles of Silly

Later, Seamus came aboard *Eibhlís* and we had an extended natter; he wrote in the logbook, 'nearly home now'. It was evident that he was excited about being almost home after the achievement of their circumnavigation. And in a gesture of pure unselfishness, to which I alluded in an earlier chapter, he offered to sail *Eibhlís* home with me and have Colmán and Kevin sail *Second Wind* on her final leg to Kinsale. I was delighted with the offer, but did not take him up on it. I could not deprive him of the last one hundred and fifty miles of his journey.

Second Wind left for Kinsale later that day and I had a decision to make. I stocked the boat next day with more fuel and fresh food and got more weather updates. I had resolved in my mind to sail the boat home on my own. Back then there were ways of organising crew to assist when boats were short of hands for a voyage but I didn't see the need for it then. Tackling the thirty-hour journey was not a big thing if the weather was not an issue, though I had to get it right in my mind as it would be the longest trip I had undertaken alone.

On a Sunday morning, 16 July, at 0830 hours, I left St Mary's behind and set course for Glandore Bay. The day was bright and sunny with a moderate wind blowing from the south-east. When I cleared the islands and looked at the vast sea ahead I felt confident but did not take anything for granted. When I was about three hours out, the wind had slacked off and I took down the foresail and motored on with the mainsail up. There was shipping in the traffic lanes and after one ship had passed well astern of me, I looked at its long hull and saw it lift and roll over the long drawn out swell that was beneath it. I was able to lash the tiller and the boat would hold its course for a good while. I occupied myself, cooking, eating, and doing laundry and sundry chores around the deck. I spliced rope and whipped untidy ends. I read and listened to the radio. The VHF was at the ready for the shipping forecast times. Dolphins appeared and kept me company for a couple of miles. Every six hours I would plot my course on the chart and top up the diesel tank from the containers I carried on board.

I was making good headway, averaging five knots, and before I knew it, it was time to put on the navigation lights for the night passage. The night was bright with a large gibbous moon and the stars were sparkling. I was keeping the North Star to the right of my starboard spreader. This obviated the need to watch the compass all the time. At 2310 hours I crossed into Irish waters and uttered a loud 'yippee'.

Into the early morning there were boats off to starboard showing lights that indicated they were trawling. I drank coffee, soup and had several snacks throughout the night to keep sleep at bay and also to distract me from my idleness. There are only so many times you can brush your teeth. The galley was spotless and every dirty sock was wrung to within an inch of its yarn before being hung on the guard rail to dry. I sang to myself and any unseen life forms in the vicinity of the Celtic Sea.

At 1220 hours on the second day, I spotted land under a hazy sky. I had wondered why it was not appearing as the GPS indicated that I was close to home. I wrote in the logbook, 'almost home now', and thought that compared with Seamus's entry on the previous page, my accomplishment was meagre.

At two in the afternoon I tied up at Union Hall Pier and had a well-earned sleep for a couple of hours. Later I met up with Tom Collins and he invited me to his house in Skibbereen for a meal. While I was near to hot water and fresh towels, I made good use of them. I met Johnny Donovan later for a few beers in Moloney's. It was after 1 a.m. when I went back to *Eibhlís* and continued the affair with my crumpled pillow. I slept until midday the following day.

I was delighted to see Liam Long in Union Hall a couple of days later; he had travelled down to sail the boat back to Dingle with me and again, like the sail around Ireland, it was a pity he missed a bit in the middle. We broke the journey in Crookhaven and once we passed the Mizen the next day we had sails filled all the way north to Dingle Bay. The voyage which had started thirty-two days before was completed with all hands home safely. *D.G.*

Chapter 8

Shuttle, Spré, Over the Water

The summer of 2007 was busier than usual for me. I was involved with three other boats apart from my own, *Eibhlís*. A boat named *Spray of Cromarty* had languished forlornly in Dingle marina for a number of years before she was rescued and given a new lease of life by two friends of mine. I had encouraged Padraig McKenna to purchase the *Spray*, now named *Spré*, and he and his brother-in-law Ciarán Crowe, who became a partner in the venture, are still talking to me in spite of the hundreds of hours spent bringing the boat back to her former graceful state, not to mind the expense involved. The boat is an old classic motor yacht of the type originally called a Gentleman's Yacht. She was built in 1928 by Thorneycroft of Southampton, a forty-foot gaff-rigged ketch with Burmese teak planking on oak ribs. It is claimed that *Spré* was one of the 'little ships' that took part in the evacuation of allied troops from Dunkirk in 1940.

Spré was in a poor state when Padraig and Ciarán took her over. Replacing the stem, mizzen mast and all the rigging were some of the major undertakings. The minor jobs were numerous and appeared one after another. I helped Padraig, who is also in the trade, with some of the work. The renovation of *Spray of Cromarty* merits a written work of its own, but that is for another day. In June of 2007 I was helping with the construction of a guardrail around *Spré's* deck. It was one of several jobs to be done before the departure deadline for the Glandore Classic Boat Regatta, which was looming. While working with the substantial teak caping for the rail, before the sharp edge had been rounded, I made a misstep while climbing over one of the fitted pieces and got a jagged scar on my shin, which I carried for the whole of that sailing season. In my own logbook for that summer there is an entry called, 'the year of the scarred shin'.

Spré gets a new stem
(etching by Deirdre McKenna)

Following the busy lead up to *Spré*'s first long voyage under the McKenna/Crowe banner, she eventually left the harbour at 1930 on 11 July, bound for Valentia Island on the first leg of her voyage. There were g-clamps on the guard rail holding scarf joints together, which were glued only hours earlier. *Spré's* crew were Padraig and his daughter Deirdre; Ciarán, his son Seamus and brother Colm; Tommy Long from Dingle, an experienced sailor who was going along as navigator and advisor to the new owners. I was sailing in *Eibhlís* with Liam Long. There was a thick wet fog crossing the bay. It was a night where the GPS was needed for entering the harbour at Knightstown. After docking at the head of the old pier at half past ten, two boats abreast, we visited the Royal Hotel and 'debriefed'. It may have been the first time Ciarán introduced the expression, which became a regular quip following our excursions at sea. After the debriefing we all retired to *Spré* for a chili con carne meal that Deirdre had brought along.

Ciarán is from Limerick and frequently visits Dingle, where his wife Helen is from. He and his son Seamus first sailed with me in 2002. When Ciarán acquired *Spré* in 2004, his daughter Róisín, who was present for the transaction, proudly announced her new appellation to the gathering on *Spré's* decks, 'I am the captain's daughter'. Ciarán has a good grasp of the topics of the day and a wide knowledge of sport, his passion being, of course, Limerick hurling. His interests are numerous and we have had several interesting conversations during our voyages together. He does not lack in humour when the opportunity arises.

At 0930 the next morning, both boats left Valentia and made for Bray Head. The wind was force three to four from the north-west and *Spré* was looking good with all of her tan-coloured sails hoisted. Our small fleet stayed close as far as Dursey, but on the long stretch between Dursey and the Mizen, *Spré* pulled away. The wind had slacked off and both vessels were motor-sailing by then. We decided via VHF radio to make off Sherkin Island and overnight there. Soon after eight o'clock that evening, *Eibhlís* berthed alongside *Spré* at the pontoon in Sherkin where Johnny Moloney, who was bound to get involved with the adventure, welcomed us ashore. Two more friends from Union Hall, Eddie Bird and Diarmuid Dineen, had accompanied Johnny to Sherkin with the intent of staying overnight with us and completing the trip to Union Hall the following morning. The voyage was shaping up to be a very agreeable undertaking. It was a good feeling being welcomed into west Cork by some of its most venerable citizens. There was much banter and stirring of 'not the spoon' ashore that night. The Union Hall trio bunked on *Eibhlís*. Eddie and Diarmuid crewed the following day with me, and Johnny, whose influence in the area extended to the 12-mile territorial limit out to sea, of course had to helm *Spré* on the way to Union Hall. After tying up at Union Hall, both crews were invited to Eddie Bird's house for lunch, where he and his wife Kath prepared a grand meal for all.

On the Saturday before the parade of sail, while boats of varying sizes, styles and aspirations were taking part in a regatta in Glandore Bay, Liam, Ciarán and I (at anchor in the middle of the visiting fleet) worked at the teak caping on *Spré's* new guard rail, shaping it by planing and sanding in preparation for the next day's event. We had an electric generator on board, which was powering the sander. I'm sure the noise we were making was not conducive to maintaining the ambience of the Glandore setting. Tommy had gone home by road with Padraig, who would be returning with his wife, Siobhán. Colm was AWOL and Seamus Crowe was trying his hand at fishing over the side. Diarmuid Dineen came aboard after whizzing around the *Spré* in his speedboat, generating a wash that he knew would annoy us. He boarded and gave moral support to all the industry emanating from the decks and then spent time fishing with Seamus, who was not having much luck in providing a fish dinner for the hard-working crew. Diarmuid was good company and very obliging anytime I visited west Cork. He will feature again in this work. After the teak rail was given a coat of oil we weighed anchor and took *Spré* for a run around the bay. Diarmuid was keen to get to know the boat and its rig some more as he would be crewing on her the following day. His knowledge of the harbour and outer bay, as well as his sailing skills, would be much appreciated by *Spré's* complement which, like that of *Eibhlís*, would not be finalised until the following morning. I know from experience, attending the parade of sail event during the Glandore Classic Boat Regatta, that you never know who is going to end up on your boat for the event. It depends largely on the company you keep the night before and the amount of people Johnny Moloney rounds up for you, unbeknownst to you, in the pub the night before. I've had Donovans, Moloneys, Nolans and many more from the area sailing with me for the colourful event, under the bunting and flags which I borrowed every two years from fisherman Bill Deasy.

The day dawned and my crew started to come to the old pier in Union Hall in dribs and drabs. I always enjoy that morning, dressing the boat before leaving the pier. The hoisting of flags and prettying the boat with colours seems to bring out the child in me and my helpers. I did it for several years before I grew disillusioned by the way our effort was never recognised by the judging committee who, as mentioned in Chapter One, gave me a prize one year for having the boat with the most unpronounceable name. But that too is another story.

We were ready for the off. *Eibhlís*'s crew was the redoubtable Liam Long, who incidentally got a fair wallop from *Eibhlís*'s wooden boom that day, partly due to the fact that space was at a premium on board; Michele Leahy from Dingle; Johnny Donovan, a native son of Union Hall whom you have heard of before in this work; and a trio of fun girls who would sail with me often: Kay, Gráinne and Eilís, who tells her friends that I called my boat after her. The surnames of the aforementioned trio are redundant in their circle as the girls have gained a particular notoriety without them. Normally we have wine and finger food on board to ward off the hunger brought on by the sea air and to add extra conviviality to the occasion. At one of the gatherings in the past we doffed hats and clinked glasses as Jeremy Irons was sailing past in a traditional west Cork boat. He reciprocated grandly as would be expected. He knew a boat of quality when he saw one.

The crew of *Spré* included four of the McKenna clan, various Crowes and Diarmuid. During the circuit of the parade our boats frequently met and there were the inevitable displays of showmanship and close-quarters manoeuvring going on. Generally the parade is colourful and has an interesting array of visiting boats, some which voyage from the south of England for the event. Galway hookers are sure to turn up as are various craft with historic connections to West Cork and its long boatbuilding tradition. Size does not matter. Classic sailing dinghies, dragons and well turned out motor boats also feature in the gathering. I was pleased to see the Tyrell-built motor vessel *Anberjenkin* from Foynes, a boat which summers in the Dingle marina, at the event in the past.

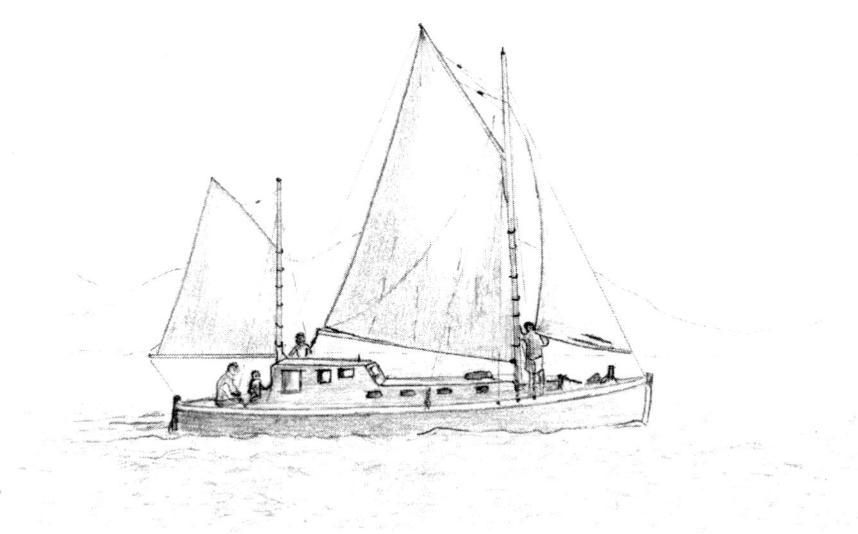

Spré under sail

The parade went on for about two hours and after we had anchored, Diarmuid provided his boat and tendered us ashore at Glandore for the prize-giving ceremony. Of all the boats competing for prizes in the 2007 parade, I would have liked to see the then eighty-year-old *Spré* get a mention, even ahead of *Eibhlís*, which, again, didn't. *Spré* is a true classic yacht with a long history and I think it behoves any organisation involved in promoting classic boats when gathering them together to support and encourage the labour involved in the upkeep of such vessels. One way of doing this is to at least recognise and applaud owners who show up with such a boat for the first time. Of course we were not in it for the prizes – most participants are not. Our reward was gathering together in our own company and enjoying camaraderie with boats and the sea as a backdrop.

Having that rant out of the way, I will now move on. Earlier in the year of the tales in this chapter, I accompanied John Griffin to the Isle of Man to check out a boat he was interested in buying. John had gone to the south of England with me when I was searching for a boat. *Eibhlís* was the result of that trip. I was returning the favour and besides John was glad to have someone with him who had a history with boats. Over the course of the weekend in Douglas, we checked out *Shuttle*, a Colvic- Watson motor sailer. John and I were happy with the boat, which had been well-kept and was generally in a sound condition. John eventually purchased the vessel and he and her previous owner had sailed *Shuttle* to Kilmore Quay. Two days after the parade of sail in Glandore, I travelled to Kilmore with John to bring *Shuttle* to Dingle. On the second leg (the first being from Douglas to Kilmore), we covered the distance from Kilmore to Crosshaven, averaging six knots. The day was pleasant with the wind off the starboard bow. We did what boats like *Shuttle* do best; we motor-sailed. It was still daylight when we pulled into the boatyard marina in Crosshaven. We strolled around the town before going for the inevitable debrief. As we walked into Cronin's Pub, the band was playing 'Dingle Bay'. How did they know we were coming?

On the third leg the next day we made off Oileán Chléire. The coastline from Kilmore was familiar to me from my trip round Ireland and the stretch from Kinsale to Oileán Chléire was well travelled by *Ployanna* and *Eibhlís*. *Shuttle* arrived into the north harbour of Cape, as it is known by many locals, to be greeted by *Spré* and her crew, who were on the return journey from Glandore. Deirdre McKenna opened a bottle of wine as soon as *Shuttle* cleared the narrow opening into the harbour. *Shuttle* got a dispensation to tie up outside the classic wooden hull. This elicited a rejoinder from John about his (GRP) boat contracting woodworm from the antique to which he was tied.

Tommy Long was also on board *Spré*, as were Ciarán and Padraig. After a cook-up on *Spré* and a practice session by me and Ciarán on two guitars, we walked to Club Chléire with instruments slung over our shoulders. The Club was chock-a-block with a gathering for a birthday party so we continued up the road to a bar that used to be Cotters in the old days. There, both our crews settled in a corner and had such a night of singing and ancillary merriment that we forgot to debrief properly.

While all of this toing and froing and singing and ancillary merriment was going on, *Eibhlís* was alone at a mooring in Union Hall harbour, though under the watchful eye of one J. Moloney. *Shuttle* and *Spré*, with their respective crews, cruised in company the next day back to Dingle. *Shuttle* was covering new ground, at least under John Griffin's ownership, and *Spré* was returning from her first long voyage south under Padraig and Ciarán's command. We had the beginnings of a cruising club in our circle. Tommy Long sailed a 'Fisher' that was also berthed in Dingle.

The next day, I got a lift back down to Union Hall and subsequently sailed *Eibhlís* home, calling to Lawrence Cove marina, which is well run by a Mrs Harrington. There is always hot water in the taps and the showers are kept clean. The marina there is sheltered in a cove and a ferry from the nearby slipway operates regularly to Castletownbere. The name of the village on the marina end of the island is Rerrin. There is a shop that carries adequate stores and next to it a pub known as Dessies, which for years had an exposed concrete floor in the bar. A couple of years ago, the floor was replaced with a wooden one; the entry in my logbook for that year reads: 'year of the new floor in Dessies'. By the way, if you are visiting Dessies, do not put your feet up on the furniture.

The third boat from the confusing title of this chapter is *Over the Water*, though that name when finally printed on her will be abbreviated to *OTW*. The lovely vessel in question is a twenty-four-foot wooden punt I set my eye on in Cahersiveen earlier that summer when on a day trip with *Eibhlís* along with Padraig. The boat is sturdy and safe and was used for inshore fishing by the previous owner; she came equipped with an outboard motor. My intention was to anchor *OTW* in the harbour at the back of my house and use her for harbour trips. The boat has since been a hit with visiting family, some of whom favour the less challenging aspects of boating.

Before the summer of 2007 ended, I took possession of *OTW* and she got a quick spin being towed behind *Spré* over the water across the bay to Dingle. Seamus Crowe, Padraig's nephew, who was on board for the trip, was happy with my acquisition. He was at the phase when he loved speed and revving outboard engines up to the very last. With Padraig's help, I lifted *OTW* out for the following winter and effected some repairs and added a few bits of my own. Eventually I would add a mast and a dipping lug rig. A friend said when he saw this: 'I knew it wouldn't be long before you put a sail on her.' She sails well going down wind and even on a broad reach she performs admirably. I use an oar over her transom for steerage. Looking at *OTW* at anchor outside my back door gives me a certain amount of joy.

Well, that was my summer of 2007, in a nutshell.

Eibhlís lift out

Chapter 9

Eibhlís's Scary Moment and an Ignominious Beach Landing; Smokey Engine and Other Stories

For the next twelve years, after the St Malo trip, *Eibhlís* stayed in home waters, mainly sailing from Dingle to West Cork, with an annual regularity that never got boring. I found that getting crew to commit to longer hauls, which would have them away from home for indeterminate periods, was difficult. I understood this, of course, and knew that I was more flexible with my time than most. There was also a bit of over-familiarity with the places to the south, within striking distance, which we had visited in the previous years. As well as that, a break from the longer journeys to explore our own coast was also desirable. I had a good pool of hands to pick from whenever I set sail from Dingle.

The following are snapshots from various cruises on the south and west coasts which are memorable to me for various reasons.

On one of those trips, Padraig McKenna was on board, as was Liam and his son Tom. Tom sailed with me and Liam often. He started when he was around twelve years of age. He was great to hold a course and engage in chat and tell stories while doing so. Sometimes he would get a touch of seasickness but yet maintain his course and stick it out till he was feeling better. He wasn't one to complain. Whenever we tied up at a marina, Tom would hose down *Eibhlís* and any other boat in its vicinity if so encouraged. On one occasion in Lawrence Cove marina on Bear Island, I asked Tom to bring a loaf of brown bread from our stores to an elderly lady who was living on her boat and I believe that after seeing his earlier industry with the water hose she would have pressed him into service willingly as crew if she got a chance.

Anyway, on this trip south, we spent a night in Knightstown, where I found that there was a charging problem with the battery. I got a second-hand replacement battery from an obliging chap on the island before we headed off. Our destination was Sneem, which is on the estuary of the River Sneem about halfway up Kenmare Bay, also known as the Kenmare River. Liam prepared smoked white trout on brown bread with salad on the way. We anchored off Garnish Island (not the one off Glengarrif), rowed ashore and walked three miles to town where we ate in Sacré Coeur. The next day as we made for Dursey, the weather was sloppy and miserable so we diverted to West Cove and dropped anchor in the small harbour. The entrance to West Cove is dodgy in bad weather. There are two large craggy rocks on either side of the fairway into the harbour. These rocks would become a worrisome duo later on. In the afternoon we went ashore and organised a taxi to Caherdaniel. We had a good meal and booked into a hostel for the night.

After coffee next morning and a look at the weather forecast, which heralded continued strong south-westerlies, we decided to go home by road for a night. Mark was driving down to collect us. But before leaving *Eibhlís* I wanted to go on board and check how her anchor was holding. When we got to the small pier in the harbour there was a fierce gusty wind blowing down the mountains into the harbour. Tom, who was behind my back said: '*Eibhlís* is moving backwards'. I said 'Tom, don't be telling fibs or I'll clip your ear', or words to that effect. Then either Liam or Padraig said that Tom was right. I looked at *Eibhlís* and saw that she was indeed making her way astern, dragging her anchor. We immediately commandeered a small punt at the pier and made haste to *Eibhlís*'s deck. Several moments of pandemonium ensued. The two large jagged rocks at the entrance to the harbour and other lesser ones that looked equally ominous were dead astern of the track that the boat was on, being blown vigorously by the squalls from the mountain. When we got on the deck I made for the cockpit to get the key and start the engine, whose battery was still not reliable. With that in mind I asked Liam and Padraig to bring lines from *Eibhlís* to a distant mooring buoy ahead. Tom helped paying out the line to the boys in the punt as they made hurriedly for the mooring. When I got the engine started after a few attempts, my crew had already reached the mooring and were making fast. While I was in the cockpit during the frenetic activity, I would look back every couple of seconds to see how we were gaining on the froth-strewn rocks behind.

Thanks to the swift action we had taken, allied with the fact that there was a punt at the ready with an outboard engine and Tom's keen eyesight, we had saved *Eibhlís* from the rocks and possibly very serious consequences. We had arrived at the pier just in time. I was reminded of

An tSiocháin's close call off the Scilly Isles in the past. A local man, Dan Casey, owned the mooring we had tied up to and he told us it was reliable and we were welcome to stay on it while we were in the harbour. After a serious fry-up on board, during which Tom was lauded as the hero of the hour, we left *Eibhlís* under the mountains and went home for a night.

***

A friend of mine from Tralee, John O'Keeffe, went on his first sailing trip with me on a fine day in early August. We had great wind off the land on the way west to the Blasket Islands. The boat was well heeled over and making good speed. John, who is a keen sportsman, was impressed with what was happening and eager to learn the ropes. He got the hang of keeping the boat on course fairly quickly. John's wife, Liz, and Kay, whom you have come across before in these pages, had decided to go on the Great Blasket by way of a ferry from Dunquin. The plan was that we would meet up with the girls there on the beach.

About a mile from the beach I downed sails and we steamed towards the shore where I tied up at a mooring owned by a local man I knew. There was a good wash crashing on the beach from the incoming tide and the gentle swell. John and I launched the dinghy and made for the beach. On the hill above, the two girls were observing our shenanigans. We didn't have to row in because the tidal motion pushed us along. When we came to the beach, a wave caught the stern of the dinghy and lifted it, turning it upside down and depositing its two occupants ignominiously onto the sand. We were drenched from head to foot and I looked up to see Liz and Kay bent over with laughter at the hilarious landing. John and I had to walk the beach in the company of the dry, wise-cracking, ferry-travelling duo for a long time before we dried off a little. We then had to lug the dinghy over rocks and hillocks to re-launch it because there was no way we could launch off the beach. When we were on the water again rowing back out to *Eibhlís*, John said to me: 'Do you do this stuff often?'

In the logbook, John described his experience as 'most enjoyable', and I have to say that I couldn't disagree with him.

***

On a trip south under engine in 2006, after leaving Portmagee Pier, I discovered exhaust fumes making their way into the cabin from the engine. The exhaust elbow from the engine to the outlet hose had pitted over time and the hole was allowing the fumes to escape. I was down below boiling the kettle and I smelled the fumes, which after a short time made me feel sick. I had to get on deck and breathe some air. I had never gotten sick on a sailing boat but it was touch-and-go that day off Puffin Island. When I started feeling a bit better I wrapped some 'Denso' tape around the elbow and it helped reduce the exit of the noxious fumes. When I got to Union Hall, a very obliging friend, Bertie, did a temporary repair job on the elbow, which saw me through the summer. I replaced the part eventually. I use this story to introduce a piece about seasickness.

I am fortunate that I normally don't get seasick. Gearoid told me once that he envied me that. In certain conditions – mostly erratic rolling of the boat when no defined motion is allowed by the sea state – Gearoid suffered from the malady, but once he gets done with it he is fine. He loves sailing so much that he accepts and endures the affliction. I have heard accounts of fishermen who get seasick every day they go to sea. It is a curious phenomenon. It is possible for an inland dweller to feel perfectly well on a sea-tossed boat while somebody reared on the harbour might not be able to abide it. I have had several of the unfortunates on board with me down through the years.

As a trip gets underway, normally in fair weather there is cheerful camaraderie in anticipation of an enjoyable voyage. There is talk and laughter, stories being told, maybe a song; snacks are consumed and general merriment prevails. After a time it is noticed that a member of the party has gone silent. There is no response when an opinion is being sought and all queries fall on deaf ears – a vacant look has replaced the hitherto happy, smiling visage. That is the first sign. Then the colour of the silent, immobile one changes to a greeny white. At this stage the rest of the group are continuing to exchange pleasantries while the transformed one is either oblivious to all or has no desire to participate lest they should have to open their mouth. All await the next development. It may come in the form of a question: 'Is there a bucket on board, John?' It may be a mad rush for the gunwale of the vessel – hopefully on the leeward side. Someone may ask the stupid question, 'Are you all right?' Any talk of food will cease as a mark of sympathy for the individual who now wishes that they were sitting under a tree in the middle of the countryside.

If one is lucky the awful feeling will pass after one has retched – if not, they are in for a horrible time until the next landfall. Eventually, when the initial jesting by the jolly, 'un-sick' crew is done, sympathy will be offered and suggestions offered as to how to feel better: 'look at the horizon'; 'don't go down below'; 'have a glass of water'. In between there will be the inevitable discussion about the best way to avoid mal de mer: wear a wrist band; take such a pill x number of hours before you sail; walk backwards onto the boat, etc. Then the wise one will suggest (as I have intimated above) that the best cure for seasickness is to sit under a tree. And when all remedies and avoiders are thrashed out, one may ask another close by: 'How do you feel?'

On a serious note, it saddens me to see anyone feeling unwell on board. To see the enthusiasm drained from them as they try to grapple with that which they have no control over is a bummer. There are a few who still sail with me in spite of the malady and I say fair play to them. A couple more have felt so helpless and horrible when stricken with it that they have had to cease the activity – that is hard, especially for those who love the idea of boats and the sea.

I don't know what works but it appears to me that the only sure-fire way for people prone to seasickness to feel well at sea is to suspend them from aloft on a gyroscopic seat – like that which holds a compass. That way the boat can pitch and roll at will while they and their last meal remain blissfully unaffected. I got sick once on a fishing boat in Dingle Bay and I have no wish to recount the circumstances of that event here other than to say that as I disembarked from the vessel at the pier in the evening, I turned to a deckhand friend of mine and said: 'You sure picked one hell of a way to make a living.'

To continue: when I left for home on the return voyage that year, Ciarán and Diarmuid joined me. We stopped outside Baltimore Harbour and Diarmuid jigged for mackerel and caught a few, which we boiled later at anchor in Schull Harbour. I am not a big fish eater because I had a surfeit of it growing up, but the mackerel, which were less than an hour out of the water, tasted better than any fish I had ever had. Diarmuid left us at Schull and Ciarán and I set sail the next day in thick fog using GPS. After an hour of clanking pots and pans, because my fog horn was not on board, the fog cleared and the wind came up. I started to haul up the main and when it was a third of the way up the halyard jammed. There was a small gap between the sheave and the mortise that contained it at the top of the mast. Sometimes when the wire halyard was allowed to fly loose, it jumped off the grooved sheave and slipped between it and the mortise, and the harder one pulled on it, the tighter it jammed. To free the halyard, a trip to the top of the mast was necessary. The first time I was hauled up to free the wire was beside the Crow Rock in Dingle Bay on a choppy sea. The motion at the top of the mast was severe and it played hell with my sense of balance and an added concern at the time was the two landlubbers at the foot of the mast who were on board for the first time and had to winch me aloft for it was in their hands that my future depended.

This time I asked Ciarán to go aloft with a screwdriver, which was required to pry out the wire from the gap. I reminded him of the old sailor's maxim, which is where the term 'hand' (in boating parlance, as in deckhand) originated: 'Keep one hand for yourself (and your own safety) and one for the boat.' The water was calm enough and there would be no excessive movement at the top. I did the winching of the bosun's chair after Ciarán was fitted with a separate safety line. Ciarán was successful in his task on high and enjoyed a spectacular view of the West Cork countryside. A couple of years later I replaced *Eibhlís*'s mast and no longer had a problem with wayward halyards.

We got the main up and sailed on to Bere Island, where we had a meal of sorts ashore before visiting Dessie in Rerrin to check out his form. Once we rounded Bray Head the next day, *Eibhlís*, on a broad reach, made eight knots on the way to the entrance to Knightstown. At nine that night we tied up at Cahersiveen Marina and hurried up town for a grand meal in An Bunnán Buí (The Yellow Bittern) at the top of the town, or is that the bottom of the town? Must ask Gráinne.

***

On the return from an overnighter to Cahersiveen a few years ago, *Eibhlís* was sailing downriver from Cahersiveen when the helmsman strayed from the channel markers and lo and behold *Eibhlís* struck ground again. This time the wait was not overlong as the tide started turning an hour after the event. One of my friends phoned home to tell of the delay (mobile phones should be banned on all boats) and the news of our grounding was in Dingle before we got home.

'Heard you went aground, John.' This I heard from an acquaintance of mine as he supped leisurely at the counter of my local in Dingle a few days later. Going aground with any boat is a no-no, a black mark against any self-respecting skipper; an ignominious position for any navigator worth his salt to find himself in; a blot in any logbook. Or so they say. Fr Gearoid said to me once: 'There are two types of sailor: those who have gone aground and those who are about to.'

How serious is it really – this striking of the bottom that results in an abrupt halt to forward motion? Well, it depends. On the larger scale with ships like the *Costa Concordia* and *Exxon Valdez* it can be catastrophic and tragic. On a small scale with, say, a ten-metre boat like mine, which has a one-and-a-half-metre draught, the probability of tragedy is negligible. How much trouble can one get into in five feet of water – that is, once the boat is sound?

Mostly, going aground is an inconvenience for a yachtsman, an embarrassment that the unfortunate one hopes will not be found out and mentioned in the clubhouse. Yachts that do strike the bottom naturally do it in shallow waters; inshore, in harbours and rivers. The ground in these locations will generally be made up of sand, mud or shale – a soft landing normally ensues, as was the case with me.

Boats are designed 'to take the ground'. Let me explain the term. Taking the ground is something you do intentionally, like drying out against a pier wall or on legs that bolt to the sides of the hull. Also, boats are designed to lie over on their sides on a strand. In Dingle on the days leading up to Easter, in the old days, the fishing boats would dry out on the strand right up against the shore for the annual painting. The hull is stiffened at the bilges to provide for this eventuality. That's taking the ground, which is allowed. Going aground is not allowed because it is done in error.

It is vital when going to sea to know about wind and tide. Invariably, the reason most sailors go aground is because they either misjudged or ignored the tides. I was mystified once to find that a man living in Dingle, albeit from a midland county originally, had no idea that the tides ebbed and flowed according to a defined pattern. 'That must make it very awkward for the fishermen,' was his rejoinder when I had explained to him the comings and goings of the sea.

What we sailors try to avoid religiously is navigating in an area of shallow water when the tide is ebbing (falling). If your boat strikes in this situation you will be stuck till the tide rises again on the flow. And depending on the state of the tide at the time of touching the bottom, one could be lodged for up to twelve hours. Or worse again, one may be 'neaped', which means a wait of several tides, or days, before the boat floats again.

When a sailor is 'stuck in the mud', he is down. He doesn't want anyone seeing him in his predicament. He wants no passers-by, who have ample water beneath their keels, waving or saluting while he wallows in his mortification. And won't that be the time when all of his boating cronies happen by as he is busies himself coiling ropes or performing some other meaningless chore, looking in the other direction all the while. I have related in this work the circumstances of my grounding near Truro and Dinan and while I was on the helm on only one of the three occasions, I must, as skipper, take responsibility for all.

So how do I answer my acquaintance who keeps a permanent shine on his corner of the bar counter with his elbows between stints, ferrying a small boat from the local pier to the harbour's mouth – a distance of one nautical mile and a bit?

'Yes, Queequeg, I did,' I say to him and as he acknowledges my admission, I add: 'I've actually gone aground in three countries.'

***

Courtmacsherry is a nice day-sail from Union Hall. I was there on my own with *Polyanna* in the years before the channel was buoyed and it was a challenging task to navigate a clear path to the pier. A floating pontoon off the pier is convenient for visiting yachts, but there is a fierce run of tide there when the flow is strong. The first time I attempted docking there, I got it wrong. I gave a good run at it from the western side, but as soon as I was alongside I was swept back by the tide before I had time to jump on and tie up. Fortunately, when I visited with *Eibhlís*, the harbour was buoyed and Liam was with me to do the jumping-off. Berthing alongside the pontoon is easier when the tides are slack.

Courtmac, as it is known locally, is very picturesque and has a nice walk along the seafront. I recently read that Courtmac is humorously referred to locally as, 'A Quiet Drinking Village with a Fishing Problem'. The harbour is open to the east but is otherwise very sheltered. The lifeboat, which was one of the first established in Ireland, is held in high regard by the community. Liam and I had a grand meal ashore and talked later with John Young, proprietor of the Pier House pub. John was welcoming and very interesting to listen to. He gave us the local history and inquired of our travels and invited discourse on a range of topics.

After our return to Union Hall, Liam travelled home and I stayed for a few more days. I called in to Baltimore on the way home, which is always busy with tourists in the summertime. After a short stay tied to the pontoon in Baltimore, I crossed the harbour and tied to a visitor's mooring off Sherkin Island.

Sherkin is a beautiful place with a scenic harbour setting that can be very tranquil in fine weather, except when high-speed boats from Baltimore cross the harbour and create noise and a large wash, which leaves boats tied up at the floating pontoon, and any moored off, dancing and bobbing erratically to the point where it becomes dangerous for people on the affected boats. I was at a mooring there once before and was nearly thrown off my deck as I tried to board my dinghy by the wash from a power boat that was rip-roaring into the cove. One is not safe down below either, especially at the cooker handling hot water and such. Sometimes the inconsiderate activity can go on into the night when the weather is fine and people are full of beans.

The island itself is interesting, with abundant wildlife and interesting walks, but I found that the warmth of welcome found in neighbouring Oileán Chléire is lacking, though there is one pub, The Jolly Roger, that makes an effort. Sherkin is like a lot of tourist places. When things are quiet there they may give you some time, but during high season, you become a number. I also got a feeling that the local boat owners wanted the harbour facilities to themselves.

North of Sherkin, on the mainland, there is a lovely village called Ballydehob, where an annual get-together of wooden boats occurs. I never got to bring *Eibhlís* there but I include it here because I made it off by road on one of my voyages to west Cork. There are none of the airs and graces about the event that can be found at other, similar gatherings. The affair is casual and the only drawback to the festival is that the location is tidal and boats with a reasonable draught have to scarper when the tide turns.

The attending boats of varying sizes are well turned out and their owners are happy to engage with the inquiring visitor. I met a student of mine from the old days, Patrick Collins, who was in the process of doing up an old ship's tender. When he started the engine, I could have stayed for hours listening to its quaint old sound.

Nicholas was with me on that visit. We had a burger cooked on the quay and we later visited a local pub up the town, which was quaint too. A jolly-looking customer sat on an unlit stove beside the counter and one could tell by his possessiveness of the steel plate beneath his bottom that it was his long-established corner of the bar.

***

How big is a voyage? How long is a piece of string? What amount of mileage constitutes a cruise? I pondered these questions before including this story and concluded that it is true to the spirit of the work. A very pleasant boat trip I had in 2012 occurred within the confines of Dingle Harbour on a fine evening in late May. It started out as a bit of a spin in a boat, but turned into a mini adventure that was enjoyed by everyone involved.

We departed from the rear of my house on the harbour in *OTW* (the harbour launch) and did a circumnavigation of the environs before ending at the mouth of the harbour, where the resident dolphin gave the usual welcoming display upon our arrival in the vicinity. My sister Bernadette, who was visiting from Adelaide, was on board, along with our brother Anthony. Padraig and Deirdre McKenna completed the adventurous quintet.

A large tree trunk had washed up on the rocks in Slaughdeen, a small cove near the lighthouse, where boys *only* gathered to swim in the old days. The cove was littered with sightseers and walkers who were enjoying the evening sunshine. A couple of smaller vessels kept our boat company on the water. The tree trunk was sizeable and denuded of bark and branches. Thousands of tiny wormholes were visible throughout its length. All of this we discovered when we approached the shore where the log rested. A small swell lapped against the craggy rocks.

I drove the boat onto the sandy beach beside the rocks and tied her off temporarily. My crew and I then traversed the uneven and weedy surface to inspect the sodden and pale-washed trunk that looked as though it had been in the water for several years. With a chainsaw we had brought along (as we had done a recon the previous evening) Padraig cut off the base of the trunk, which was flared out and still had some of the larger root tentacles attached. It would have been very difficult to tow with that lot still in place.

It was an all-hands-on operation with Bernadette and Deirdre in the thick of the operation. When it came to rolling the log from the rocks onto the surf, it took the full complement of our crew to get it moving. Having Anthony along was a boon. After several attempts at rocking the stubborn tree trunk back and forth to get momentum, we got it into the water and lashed some ropes to it, but the battle was not over. When we brought the boat around and took the lines, the wash kept floating the log back onto the rocks. Padraig got onto the rocks again and rolled the log while I pulled on the lines with the outboard engine on high power. Another boat close by offered assistance but we were determined that this huge chunk of driftwood from God knows what part of the world would not get the better of us.

After much human and mechanical grunting, the log floated off finally and the boat pulled it clear. Padraig walked along the shore to a spot more suitable for getting back on board. We then made slow progress under engine back to base but happy with our success. It was an especially enjoyable adventure for Bernadette, who had not played or got up to devilment in the harbour for many years.

I left the log on the strand at the back of my house and over the winter months I cut it up for firewood; the innards were riddled with large worm holes and the tunnels they had bored through stank something terrible. After sawing and chopping it into stove-sized chunks, I washed the pieces in barrels full of fresh water and then lay them out to dry for weeks.

There is a punchline to this story and it's partly why I have included it. Following the adventure, I was recounting the story to a friend of mine: 'Sounds like a lot of work, John,' he said, and added, 'if it was fuel you wanted, wouldn't it be a lot easier to buy a couple bags of coal?'

To my way of thinking there was only one answer to that, which I uttered with profound glee: 'Sure, anybody could do that'.

Chapter 10

Tall Ships and Small Ships

The smell wafting from *Eibhlís's* galley as she made her way down the south-west coast in 2011 to join the tall ships was like that which assails one when passing a high-street restaurant of renown. Liam was at the cooker preparing caramelised garlic and meat cutlets, which would be served with stir-fried potatoes with chorizo. A cabernet sauvignon was at the ready to accompany the meal. Deirdre McKenna and I were in the cockpit awaiting the outcome of the industry playing out below decks – the smell was driving us crazy. On leaving Dingle we had decided to sail overnight and make Crosshaven on the first leg. Liam's cooking hit the spot, as always, and fortified us for the long journey. We were bound for the Waterford estuary for the parade of tall ships a couple of days hence.

Fastnet Lighthouse

The next evening we were wined and dined by Liam's nephew, Michael Kavanagh, and his wife Valerie, in Crosshaven before we departed for Dungarvan, which would be our staging spot for the tall ships event. In Dungarvan we ate well ashore. It is no wonder that at the end of each summer I have added pounds from indulging at the table, especially when Liam is crewing. Anytime he eats, I feel that I have to as well. Deirdre always brings along a cooked meal when she is crewing and that never fails to go down well too, though she and other women who have crewed with me are a bit shy of the washing-up lest the activity be seen to reinforce the old-fashioned expectation, to which I say: if a man is willing to do it, why not a woman? But Deirdre has other talents too. She is an artist and I am happy to own two of her works, both of which have a nautical theme. Following a voyage to La Coruña, in Spain, on the *Jeanie Johnston* some years ago, Deirdre's work had a nautical theme and she produced some remarkable pictures representing life on a sailing ship.

Dungarvan Harbour dries out at low tide. There is a pontoon beside the pier wall where yachts can tie up once they are willing to take the ground, which is soft mud. *Eibhlís* sank into the mud by about two and a half feet and remained relatively upright. My crew and I sampled the nightlife in the town and retired early to be off with the tide in the morning. At 0710 hours we departed and made for the Waterford estuary to see the ships exit to the sea. We arrived at the estuary in time to see the first of the ships sail out. We mingled and weaved between the fleet. The day was fine but a little more wind would have given purpose to the thousands of acres of canvas on display.

The *Asgard II*, which was lost in the Bay of Biscay three years previous, would normally lead the fleet of tall ships when the event was held in Irish waters but alas those days were over and as I write there are no plans afoot to replace the majestic sail-training vessel which was home to thousands of young sailors over the course of twenty-seven years. I thought to myself as I watched the representative ships from all over the world, where is the *Jeanie Johnston* or the *Dunbrody*? Is there any noble vessel in Ireland willing to lead these ships on their onward journey in the country they chose for a host? I understand that the latter ships are not sail-training vessels as such, but there were plenty of (small) Irish boats amidst the tall ships fleet that day, including *Eibhlís*, marking the event and showing hospitality to the ships that were thousands of miles from home. We had no boat with the majesty of *Asgard II* to see the majestic fleet on their way. *Celtic Mist* had led the fleet out of the Waterford estuary but she just didn't cut the mustard.

As the ships headed for Greenock in Scotland, *Eibhlís* set a course for the Old Head of Kinsale.

Back in Union Hall the following day, Johnny Moloney and I visited Eddie Bird's house, where a stove was being fitted and there was a debate bordering on hilarity as to the position of the stove relative to the original fireplace opening. Johnny wanted it fitted into the opening and Eddie wanted it halfway in, or maybe it was the other way round. I was asked for an opinion but thought it was wiser to just observe. Though it was Eddie's house and Eddie's call, Johnny was not happy until the job was done the way he wanted. It was typical of the relationship the two friends had. Johnny demanded and Eddie acquiesced for the sake of a quiet life.

Eibhlís took part in her last Parade of Sail (under my command) in Glandore a few days later and space was again at a premium with several local and Dingle friends on board. The day was blowing hard and some thrilling moves were experienced by one and all – and again, no prize. Sailing home that year Diarmuid came as far as Cape, where we stayed overnight. Padraig and Fergal Cunningham, a colleague of mine, sailed the boat from Cape to Valentia Island in thick fog for most of the next day. We docked in Portmagee for the night and I continued as the cruise had begun: indulging in excellent cuisine, this time in the The Moorings Restaurant, where, when we arrived late, the management accommodated us willingly.

Chapter 11

Back to Killary

I had not sailed north of Dingle Bay since I sailed around Ireland with Liam in 1999. My inclination when leaving the bay has always been to go south. Old Boreas continues to assist me in my sailing endeavours but wants to keep pushing me south. During the years making off destinations south of Bray Head there was but one place to the north which occasionally and increasingly crossed my mind, a place I had visited just once and found to be beautifully scenic and somehow calming to my spirit, a place where I felt very much at home, but while the feeling I experienced when I first sailed in there was perhaps fleeting, as the years passed I felt myself being pulled back there to see again, or feel again, whatever it was that attracted me to the place. When I sailed around Ireland in 1999, I gave this place I speak of a miss for various reasons – one possibly being that I considered it a destination in its own right, a place to savour rather than a quick stopover.

I mentioned earlier in this work Fr Gearoid's favourite place, the Island of Iona, and I believe that many people have places where they are at ease and comfortable though some may not understand the pull or the draw of that place. More than two decades after my first visit to where I now call my 'soul place', I went back on *Eibhlís* in 2012 and followed the track of *An tSiocháin* twenty-two years earlier into the long stretch of water between the mountains of counties Galway and Mayo. This trip would also be the last significant voyage of *Eibhlís*, but more about that later.

Liam had gone back to the land. He tended animals and bees on a small farm west of Dingle. He found it harder to get away for the annual sailing trip either because of the commitment to his newfound friends or the desire to get away from the regime aboard boat, which included having my shoes polished each morning and presenting me with a precisely cooked three-minute egg.

Tom McCarthy, who had done some local sailing with me in the bay and had developed a *grá* for sailing on a trip on board the *Jeanie Johnston* to Spain in 2007, was keen to do an extended voyage along the Irish coast so he was all on for the trip north. Barry, whom you have come across earlier, a colleague from my college days and the illustrator of this work, also signed up for the voyage. We set off on the evening of 3 July and were through the Blasket Sound before nightfall. The wind was slack and the night was sloppy, almost identical to the night when *Eibhlís* last had Loop Head abeam. At 1100 hours the next day we sailed through the Gregory Sound and rounded to Kilronan Harbour where we picked up a mooring buoy which we found later to be free for visitors. After a bite of grub (note the description of the food now that Liam was absent from the galley) and a few hours' sleep, we went ashore and came across a group from Tralee Sailing Club who had docked earlier. They were better equipped for merriment than we were as they had a guitar and were bound for a sing-song in Tí Joe Watty's.

Barry cooked breakfast in the morning before we left for Inishbofin. Tom was enjoying the trip and delighted in helming *Eibhlís* along the coast while he regaled us with stories from his voyage to Spain. It was his and Barry's first real test of *Eibhlís*. As the trip progressed they would learn more about her capabilities. The coastline was familiar to me but my new crew were taking it all in. At 1955 hours we dropped anchor in Inishbofin Harbour after making a complete codswallop of an attempt at berthing beside the eastern pier. An old boy looking at us from the shore was shaking his head in disgust at our incompetence. He was not aware of *Eibhlís's* stubbornness when motoring astern. The night had grown very wet. We rowed ashore and had a meal in Days Bar. Later two locals were having a conversation at the bar and one asked the other: 'Are you walking or do you have wipers?' The solution to this riddle was that many of the cars on the island were 'bangers' and didn't have windscreen wipers and on such a wet night a car without wipers was useless, hence 'Are you walking ...' Get it?

The following morning, unbeknownst to my crewmen, I was excited when we weighed anchor and started making our way east towards Killary. After all the years of promising myself that I would return, I was about to see again the spot where I had spent just a short period of time and yet had yearned for so long to return to by boat. Going back there by road would not have been the same. I had to see the fjord from the sea again and I hoped to recapture the sense of awe I felt in 1990.

Eibhlís made her way east with Tom at the helm while Barry familiarised himself with the navigation, making sure that every rock was where it was supposed to be. The way east was strewn with outcrops of stones and small islands. After passing Inishlyon we changed course to the north-east and left Crump Island and the O'Mallybreaker to starboard, then we stayed south of Carrickgaddy Rocks which were 2 miles from the entrance to the fjord. Our navigation had to be keen as the visibility was not great. About a mile from the entrance, the gap became visible. South of the entrance there is a strip where Little Killary Harbour is snugly wedged into a corner. After leaving that behind we were into the fjord.

The wind was moderate with a northerly aspect and, just like the first time I was there, intermittent gusts would rush through the mountain gaps on the Mayo side and *Eibhlís* would heel a bit more as she picked up speed. Boreas was greeting us again. The visibility had improved and we could see the layout of the fjord quite well. Apart from strings of mussel farms along the southern (Galway) side of the channel, the place was much as I remembered it. From the deck of the boat, the mountains on the Mayo side appeared steeper and more imposing than their neighbours across the water.

Killary Harbour viewed from the entrance

As we made our way along I could see that my companions were also impressed with the wonder of the place. Whether it was doing anything for their inner souls, I could not say. I felt like I had left something behind when I last visited and was back to retrieve it. The ten-mile stretch of water was gliding past us by the minute and I somehow wished the journey along the side of the mountains would last longer. The first two thirds of the fjord are about a constant seven hundred yards wide and close to a true south-east course. The final third bends to due east and narrows off. On reaching the village of Leenane at the eastern end, the view looking back is spectacular. We picked up a visitor's mooring on the western side of the village. The location was not conducive to a lot of coming and going in the dinghy so we decided to stay ashore for the night. There was a major emergency when Barry lost his phone on the trek to the village and I was not helpful when I told him that by and large phones could be done without. Tom saved the day when he found the phone resting on a wall and then two thirds of the crew were happy again. We had showers in the local hotel and a meal before booking into the convent for the night – The Convent B&B. We later made off to the pub, where I had watched the Ireland/Italy match in 1990, and had a few scoops.

Leenane: Barry, John and the Bull McCabe (background)

The dining room of the B&B was the original chapel of the convent and there we were served up a decent breakfast the next morning. The setting of the building allowed me to look out onto the fjord and see *Eibhlís* at her mooring in the distance. The Convent was well run, with nary a habit in sight, and good value for money. It had an interesting library on the ground floor if only one had time to explore its shelves, but we were sea-bound folk and anxious to be under sail again. After shopping in the village we went back to *Eibhlís* and slipped her from the mooring line.

Sailing out along the fjord, we were sheltered from a strong northerly wind, which gave us a blast as soon as we cleared the entrance. We were bound for Clifden and for the next three hours we would have spectacular sailing while travelling more than 180° around the compass and implementing six different sail settings. For the first seven miles we sailed west on a beam reach and clocked up eight knots for a time. We were retracing our course of the day before for a part of the way. The second course, on a broad reach, took us on a middle path between Inishbofin and the mainland, ending north of Cuddoo rock. There we eased off the main further and stayed on the verge of a gybe for two miles as far as the gap between Friar and High islands, then we gybed and went on a run till we were south of Cruagh Island where a south-easterly course took us as far as Carrickrana Rocks. After that, a course slightly north of east, the final leg, brought us into Clifden Harbour.

The reason I have detailed that journey so well is because Barry has it all marked clearly on the chart we used. The compass bearings and the length of each track are included. We could have done it in the dark or thick fog with the aid of the GPS as we used both visual and electronic information. Tom steered the complete course with instructions from Barry while I mainly changed the sails. Given the conditions, the exercise was ideal for a sail-training lesson. I enjoyed it immensely and remarked to my crew that it was the best bit of sailing *Eibhlís* had done in a long time.

The harbour in Clifden is about a mile out from the town. There we anchored for the night and again, due to the trek into town, or rather out of town late at night, we opted for a B&B. We were really spoiling ourselves. On the walk in, Tom met a first cousin of his who was holidaying in the area. We had a great meal in a local restaurant and visited a couple of hostelries. Barry and I reminisced in the Alcock and Brown Hotel about the time we had spent in the town when on an Irish course in Connemara in the late seventies. A lot of water had passed under our keel since those days. We also found a pub where a party was in progress. Before the end of the night I commandeered a guitar and Barry sang his own version of 'Willie MacBride'.

We started on the homeward journey the next morning and with sails full all the way we averaged six knots over the journey to Kilronan where we anchored overnight. We set out early the following day for the Blasket Sound. The wind was blowing fresh from the north-west and as the day got going the sea built up a bit. *Eibhlís* was getting walloped in the starboard quarter by the occasional extra-large lump of water and one of the same knocked Tom off the steering perch on the high side. It took Tom awhile to get used to going to port momentarily when the large ones were coming so that the boat's stern would lift and ride the oncoming sea. In such conditions, it is prudent for the helmsman to look behind from time to time to see the building waves. The last time I had sailed south on that coarse was on *Polyanna* and the conditions at the time were similar, but *Eibhlís* was far more robust, weightier and stable for the wind and sea on the day.

Cooking a decent meal was not on so we made do with sandwiches and coffee. The day had turned grey with rain threatening but staying at bay. The weather forecast for later in the day was for strengthening westerly winds and I reckoned we would be in the vicinity of the Blaskets when that occurred. We were getting a small bit weary of the ride south and after six hours of it I decided we would make for Tralee Bay and the port of Fenit rather than go through the Blasket Sound in worsening conditions. It was a decision that came easy. We were not in such a hurry that we felt we had to suffer a pasting around Sybil Head in heavy seas. We tied up in Fenit after being ten hours out. I noticed Fr Gearoid's *Aqua Viva* berthed beside us but alas nobody was home. We travelled home by road and took a break for a day or two, returning later to sail *Eibhlís* home on a fine warm though windless day.

***

I will remember that voyage north for the new crew of course and for the great sail we had from Killary to Clifden. I will also remember it as *Eibhlís's* last significant voyage under my command. But I will remember it most for bringing me back to Killary fjord again. What is it about that place?

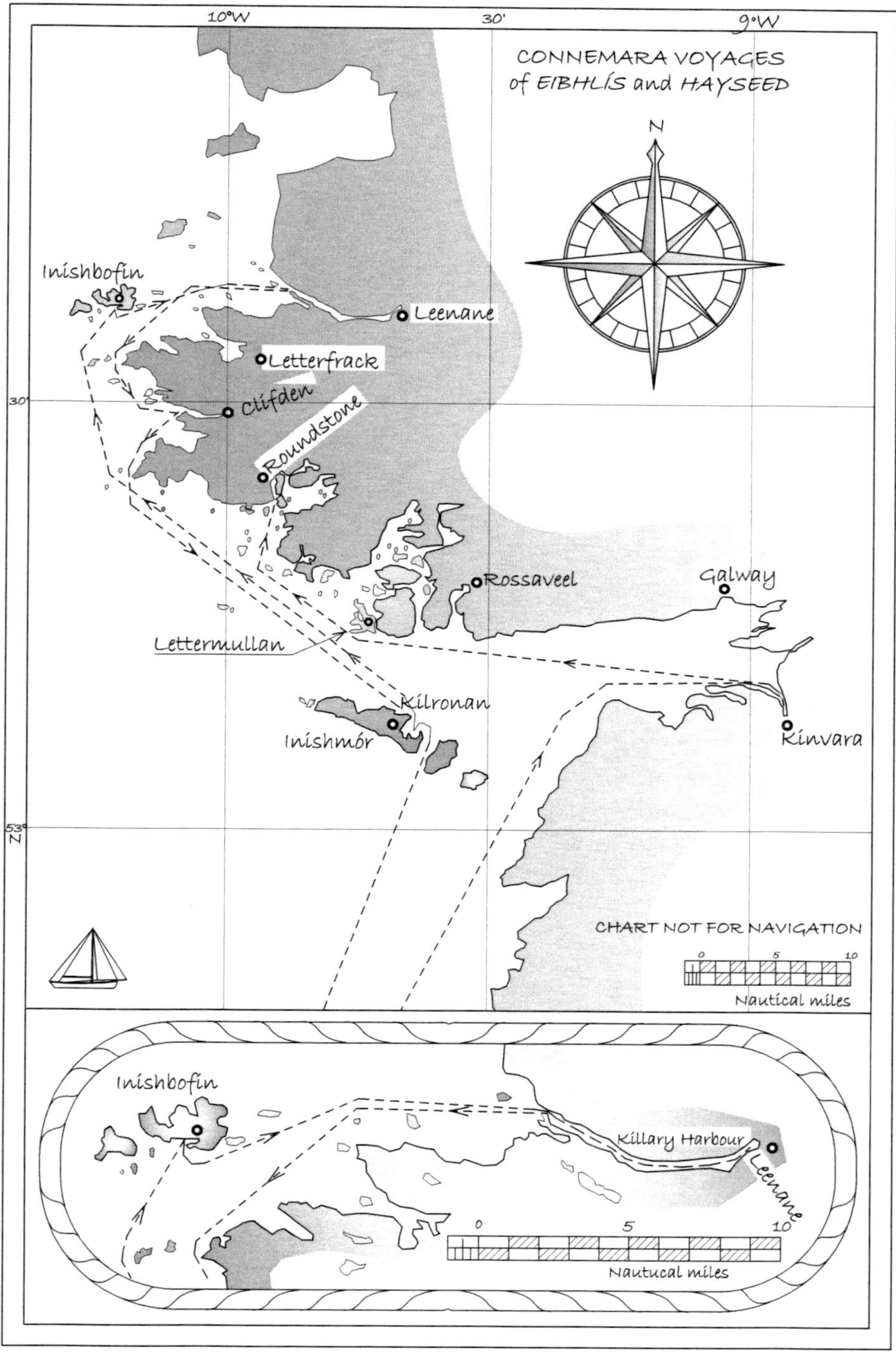

10°W
30'
9°W
CONNEMARA VOYAGES
of EIBHLÍS and HAYSEED
N
Inishbofin
Leenane
Letterfrack
30'
Clifden
Roundstone
Rossaveel
Galway
Lettermullan
Kilronan
Inishmór
Kinvara
53°
N
CHART NOT FOR NAVIGATION
0
5
10
Nautical miles
Inishbofin
Killary Harbour
Leenane
0
5
10
Nautucal miles

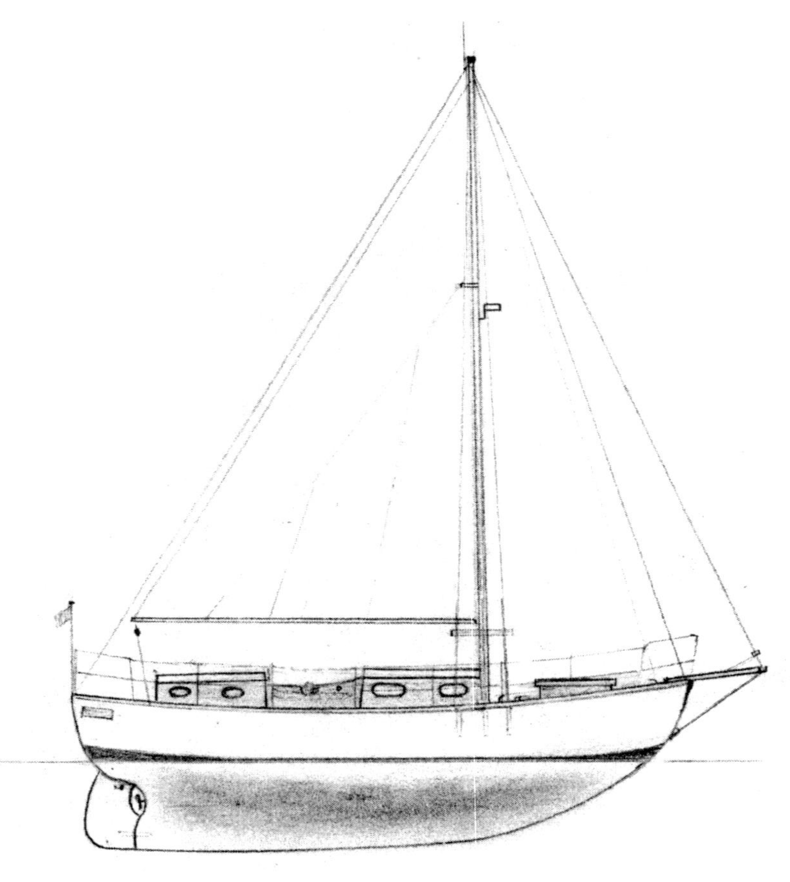

Part Four

Hayseed

Chapter 1

ON 308° ONCE AGAIN

In the autumn of 2012 I began searching for my next boat. I had in mind to get a motor sailer, which is a vessel with a more powerful engine than the more conventional yacht and a wheel house to provide shelter in bad weather. A motor sailer also carries sails, normally on two masts, hence their being ketch rigged. Many sailors, when they tire of hauling up sails and getting drenched wet in open cockpits, opt for the motor sailer, which they use more often than not as a motor boat. An internet search of popular boat sites revealed several boats of the length and price range I was interested in, but they were predominantly made of fibreglass. I was not, in spite of hints and taunts from friends in the sailing fraternity, prepared to abandon wood for plastic.

My quest took me first to Aberystwyth in Wales where a Miller Fifer was on offer. The boat was structurally sound but needed a good bit of cosmetic attention. I was not looking for a major project. The hours I had spent over sixteen years keeping *Eibhlís* looking good had taken a certain toll. This time I was willing to pay extra for a boat that was ready to go with minimum initial work. I knew that any wooden boat I got would require upkeep, but I wanted to start ahead of the posse. A friend told me once that he couldn't understand why I accepted the burden of keeping a wooden boat so easily and kept going back to them again and again. My reply was somewhat philosophical but I believe I meant it: 'I would rather the burden than live while cruising in a plastic world.'

The next stop in what many would describe as my ludicrous pursuit was Arklow, home of a famous boatyard, Tyrrell's, that has produced numerous seaworthy fishing vessels and motor yachts for more than one hundred years. A motor sailer, one of four built by the yard, was for sale and its provenance alone steered me to look it over. It was a fine-looking boat with many of the hallmarks of the Tyrrell yard but alas it too would need a good bit of cosmetic work before I would be able to use her. After perusing the internet further, I was beginning to despair about not finding what I wanted, but after some urging from friends who were surprised to hear that I was going to leave pure sailing behind, I was prompted to think again.

I travelled to England with Nicholas in early 2013 to look at two Hillyards: wooden yachts built by another reputable company, Hillyards of Littlehampton. The nine-tonner of the series, being thirty-two foot on deck, was the one I was interested in. The two boats were within ten miles of each other in Torpoint, Cornwall, opposite the city of Plymouth. The first one I looked at was a let-down. It needed a bit of structural work. *Hayseed*, the second vessel, which I now own, looked very appealing to me when I first saw her on the hard. Though she was fifty years old, it was obvious that she had been kept well. The main features of *Hayseed* that differed from *Eibhlís* were a centre cockpit, a double-ended stern and a bowsprit, which allowed the boat to be cutter rigged. The interior layout was well done and the centre cockpit gave room for an aft cabin. The underwater profile was long keel with a good draught. A 40-horsepower Mercedes engine, though old, was in great condition and gave the boat an appealing charm with its 'old sound'.

The owners at the time, Rupert and Susie, were reluctant to part with the boat, but a health issue was part of the reason they were downscaling to a more manageable sailing boat that demanded less upkeep.

I had an independent survey completed on the boat. When I read the report, which was very positive, I made an offer. Rupert and I also made a deal that he would antifoul and launch the boat for me before I took possession. After launching, Rupert and Susie came on board with me and we spent an hour sailing in Plymouth harbour so they could familiarise me with the workings of the boat and point out any features that were specific to *Hayseed*. As they bade farewell to the boat, I could see that the previous owners were reluctant to let her go on the one hand and glad to see that someone with a love for wooden boats had bought her.

A chain (cable) ferry operates between Torpoint and Devonport and has done so since 1831. Anyone with an interest in engineering will be fascinated by the workings of these ferries, of which there are three, with each having a capacity for seventy-three cars. The crossing is about 650 metres and takes between three and four minutes; there are two slipways on either side, which accommodate at all stages of the tide. Seeing the huge chains get swallowed up as they make their way to the innards of the vessel where two large chain wheels, each nearly two metres in diameter, grab them and move them along makes one marvel at the ingenuity of the design. Of course the chains are not moved along; they are anchored at each shore. It's the ferry that travels along the chains, one port and one starboard. After the chain exits the stern of the ferry, it sinks to the seabed so that other ships can use the estuary at the mouth of the river Tamar. An interesting thought: as these ferries never turn around, 'forward' and 'astern' changes depending on the direction of passage. That must mean that two sets of port and starboard navigation lights are available for night passage.

I spent most of a week on my own getting *Hayseed* organised for the trip home. I visited a couple of charity shops and bought delph, cutlery and other galley items. In a chandlery in Plymouth I purchased a new life raft and a stainless steel cooker which replaced the basic one ring that came with the boat. As I travelled back and forth to the ferry I would stop often and look at a lovely old wooden boat of the harbour-launch type that was standing dry forlornly on the hard. I imagined that if she came with words it would be: 'Take me home'. But for the impracticalities of the location and the attention to my higher mission, I would have inquired into her ownership and intent. I've come across old and abandoned wooden boats down through the years and it has occurred to me that their neglect is suffered by their owners rather than seeing them broken up for firewood. We used to have a graveyard of old fishing boats in Dingle harbour, which proved to be an attraction for many visitors. The boats were abandoned on the shore when they had fulfilled their usefulness. In time their decks collapsed and their ribs exposed themselves to the elements. Over a longer time their components dissolved into the ground from whence they came. It was the end the owners desired – using a chainsaw to speed up their demise would not be considered. So whenever I see a recoverable craft I entertain wishful thoughts of injecting new life into its veins. As I write there is such a project awaiting my attention.

Looking for a home?

There was a decent restaurant on the marina grounds where the boat was docked and I had a couple of good meals there. A conversation I overheard between two men while dining one night went like this:

'Ye, she finally laid down the law to me. She said it was either her or Wendy.'

The other man responded: 'Well, you asked for it, I suppose. You were hardly ever home in your free time. Women can only take so much of that.'

'Looks like I'll have to give her up after all these years. It won't be easy.'

'How long have you and Wendy been an item?'

'Nearly twenty years now.'

'And there is no chance she will accept that Wendy is part of your life too?'

'I have tried, believe me, but she said I have had it both ways for too long'.

I was surprised that such a conversation continued within earshot of my table and at some stage started getting suspicious. Later in the conversion I deduced that Wendy was a wooden boat and probably named *Windy.*

In early May I brought a crew over to sail the boat home, but northerly gales persisted for over a week in southern England and on the shipping areas we would be crossing. Reluctantly I advised the crew that we should all go home and wait for a better chance.

Towards the last week in May the weather was forecasted to settle a bit and I contacted Barry to see if he would be able to fly to England with a couple of days' notice. He said there would be no problem with that. I had no intention of organising a larger crew in case I had to postpone again. After three days in Torpoint, waiting again and stocking up with rations, Barry and I finally got away on the 22 May, I never wanted to get out of a marina so much. Getting *Hayseed* out of the marina through the narrow opening was my first trepidatious task. The extra five foot of a bowsprit was also something I would have to get used to when manoeuvring in the confines of a marina. We had to call into a fuelling berth in another marina, Mayflower Marina, before we left Plymouth Harbour. The less said about going alongside the fuelling berth against an outgoing steam, the better. The man operating the fuel station had great fun looking at the two Irishmen who told him they were making for Ireland.

I was glad to get out into the open sea where I could get a proper feel for *Hayseed* and how she responded to the controls and of course to haul up sail and see what she was made of. I was not disappointed. On the run from Plymouth to Lizard Point we had a strong north-westerly blowing and Barry and I were well pleased with *Hayseed's* performance. She was steady and answered well to the sails we had hoisted. She was every bit as good as *Eibhlís* and I couldn't have asked for more. Once we rounded the Lizard the wind was on our nose all the way to Newlyn Harbour. It was a three-hour slog under engine and main to the entrance.

Thirteen years had passed since I had been in that neck of the woods and on entering the harbour I saw that a marina had been installed since then. We found a convenient berth upon entering and after tying up we sought immediately to christen the first leg of *Hayseed's* voyage to her new home. I had forgotten the lay of the land and we walked off in the wrong direction after getting to the top of the pier. We found a pub that was still open and said 'cheers' while the jukebox played numbers from our younger days. The next day I got my bearings. To me the whole place looked like it hadn't gotten a lick of paint since I was last there. The people hadn't changed. They were friendly and accommodating as before. Barry and I got to know artist-in-residence Ben Gunn, whose claim to fame (at the time) was a painting of some of the rocks on the marina breakwater. Ben took us to his studio where he had a large selection of paintings on display, most of them seascapes and coloured sky combinations. We became friends with Ben and his partner during our stay. They were welcoming and good fun to be with. Ben wore a chain with a gold key around his neck, which had something to do with a long lost love though we never got the full story.

While the weather suited the trip from Plymouth to Newlyn, it was far too unsettled to be heading north so we had to wait a couple of days for the off. I checked out Penzance again, this time with Barry, and it too was much the same as before. On the night before we left Newlyn, we had a crowd of fishermen around us in the pub as we looked at weather forecasts on our mobile devices. Their input was welcome though varied as to tackling Land's End on the following day. One fisherman told us he had been out there that morning and that the waves had been high and challenging. While he said it he looked up at an invisible wave beyond the ceiling. Another looked at us with a funny look that seemed to say, 'Do you guys know what ye are doing?' Of course, they had no idea how many sea miles we had under our belt.

We weren't quite sure how to take their suggestions as the following night was a big night in the pub and they wanted us to stay for it. On the morning of 25 May, we untied our lines as a moderate wind blew and I left Newlyn behind once again. It was my sixth time sailing out of that harbour. We headed for Land's End. The day was fine and the wind had eased a lot, blowing off the land as we made for the Runnel Stone cardinal mark off the southern corner of Land's End. The coastline was getting familiar to me as we progressed and Barry was taking in every mile along the way. At Land's End the water was flat with a gentle swell spread out over the area. After rounding, we saw the Longships Lighthouse off to starboard. This lighthouse marks an area of foul ground situated over a mile west of the mainland.

Longships lighthouse

We left the Isles of Scilly well off to port and the Longships behind us and set a compass course of 308° for Glandore bay. I didn't think in the preceding years that I would be voyaging in these waters again and somehow it was good to be back and in the company of someone to whom the whole thing was new. The last time I had crossed the Celtic Sea from the Scilly Isles, I had been on my own.

Hayseed was fitted with an auto-helm, which was as good as another man once we got used to its workings – and we didn't even have to water or feed it. Barry wanted to be involved in all the navigation as he was keen to learn more about it. That was fine with me. Having someone like him on board was a joy compared to some who would be asking after a few hours out, 'How long will it take?'

The wind had slacked off quite a bit and we were motor-sailing at about six knots. I didn't care about not having wind. My main concern was to get *Hayseed* home safely to Ireland by any means. There would be plenty days for sailing without the noise of the engine in the future, *le cúnamh Dé*. At 1915 hours, Barry prepared a meal of chicken kebabs, carrots and potatoes, which fortified us for the night ahead. Coldness was setting in and through the night plenty of hot drinks would be required.

Sailing through the night was a big event for Barry and he was enjoying the experience. A spectacular moon rose out of the water directly behind our stern and climbed like a red ball in the beginning. Later, it brightened and shone on the shimmering water. But if we thought that was a remarkable happening, what we saw at dawn outdid it considerably. The sunrise presented the most spectacular combination of sea and sky I had ever seen at sea. The golden amber colours infusing the water and scattered clouds above resulted in a truly magnificent picture of the natural world at its best. After the ball of the sun had cleared the horizon, it was obscured by a cloud bank for a while before it rose as if for the second time to burst once more into the atmosphere. And like the show the moon put on, this was all for us. There was not another vessel in sight.

Moon on the wake

I always make room for books on board my boats. When I had *Polyanna*, whose space down below was in much demand, I still managed to squeeze in a couple of hardbacks. When *Eibhlís* came along, I was able to commandeer a decent section of shelving for my novels and reference books and with *Hayseed* I have similar luxury. My love of books extends beyond the obvious enjoyment that the actual reading gives. I also love to see books on a shelf, arranged in an orderly fashion, with their spines proclaiming a hint only of what lies between the dusty covers. I can understand how they are used ornamentally to enhance a room's decor. But I find them a comfort just having them at hand in case something unexpected befalls me whereby I have to wait out a situation without recourse to any other form of pastime. I have the one which begins: 'Call me Ishmael', naturally, and others of similar vein; there is always a smattering of quick-read who-dun-its onboard as well as the required reference books and almanacs.

After my good friend and sailing companion, Len Breewood, died in 1999, his wife Margaret showed me all of his nautical books and told me to take any or all that I wanted from his collection. I have some of his books on board and in my home library also. So whenever there is a long stretch of water to be traversed, the boat work is in order and I have a trustworthy pair of hands to 'take the con', I love to stretch out in my bunk, where my mini-library is at hand, and switch off for a time.

At around noon we spotted land in the distance. This coincided with a freshening wind developing from the south-west. We hauled up the foresail (the main was already in play) and switched off the engine and had a good sail for the last four hours of the passage. As we got closer, Galley Head became visible to starboard. Barry said to me, 'You must have done this before', a comment on the accuracy of the navigation, but in truth with modern navigation aids it is not a big deal. When sailing on *An tSiochâin* in the eighties it would have been a cause for back-slapping.

The following morning Barry and I were awakened at Union Hall Pier by Johnny Moloney and a contingent who were there to inspect the new vessel. We were bleary-eyed and unprepared for visitors following a few celebratory beers the night before and then the most welcome state of unconsciousness after our long passage awake at sea. The welcome was typical of my Union Hall cronies. After some light banter we all repaired to Rosscarbery for brunch. Barry left for home later that day as I had decided to stay a couple of days in west Cork before completing the voyage. In the evening I visited uncle James, Johnny's uncle, and was served the best tea in all of County Cork.

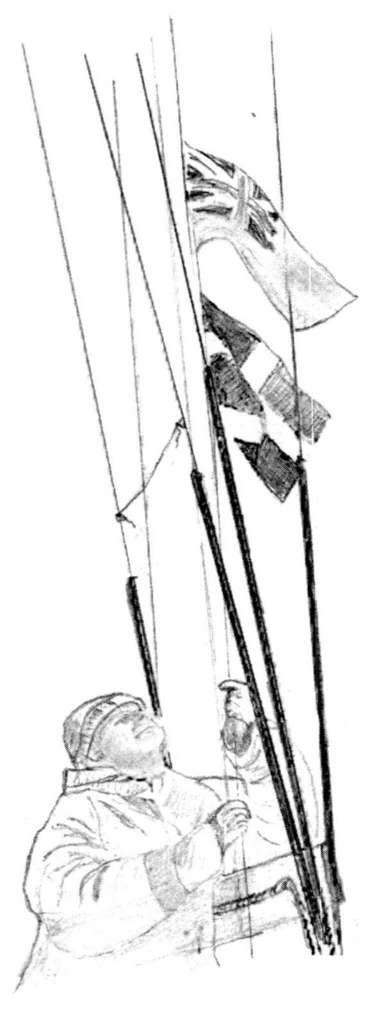

Back in Irish waters

The homeward voyage of *Hayseed* continued some days later with Barry, Tom McCarthy and Kiera McKenna. We overnighted outside the ferry on Oileán Chléire. A meal of curried stew was served up with fresh bread that Tom had bought in Macroom on the drive down – more about the bread later. We made the obligatory visit to Club Chléire before settling down for the night. There we met Tommy and Connie Cadogan who filled us in on the latest goings-on in the area. At nine the following morning we left Cape with the intention of making off Valentia Island but it was a hard slog after the Mizen. A strong north-westerly had built up a bit of sea and we were not making much progress motor-sailing. We decided to head for Bear Island. After rounding the Mizen and getting Sheep's Head on our beam we had a great sail on the north-easterly course to the eastern end of the island.

Kiera cooked a beef stroganoff dinner on board and the gas ran out soon after. There was no gas available on the island and the prospect of the long haul the next day without hot drinks was not agreeable to the crew. Sometime later I remembered the stowed one-ring camping stove that had come with the boat. After checking it out I found it had about a half a canister of gas left, so we were assured of our coffee fix the following day. We visited Dessies' pub and chatted with the proprietor, who was all talk for a change – must have been because I was in the company of a Cork man, Barry.

Sailing west off the land from Castletownbere Harbour to Dursey Island, *Hayseed* was well heeled over by the brisk wind that was blowing from the north-west. Tom was at the wheel enjoying the ride. The sea had a good chop worked up and keeping the course demanded keen attention. After passing Blackball Head, Tom asked Barry if he would fire up the coffee pot. Tom had given a gift of a pot for making 'proper' coffee to the boat when we were shopping in Plymouth before the postponed trip home. Barry suggested that due to the rough ride we were having that we wait until we were in the lee of Dursey on the way to the sound. *Hayseed* ploughed on and before long was rounding the Cat Rock and making for the sound. The sea flattened out and we all waited for the passage through the gap beneath the cables. No matter how often I go through the sound, it is always a good talking point for the crew of the day. On exiting on the northern side we were met by a very lumpy sea and a wind on the nose, as expected. We would be making slow progress north. Over an hour later we were abeam Scariff Island and Tom still had not got his coffee.

The sea was glistening from the bright sun, which was laying a layer of bronze on our faces. There was an invigorating freshness in the air. We motor-sailed doggedly on for Puffin Island and then Bray Head and longed for the sail up Dingle Bay as soon as we rounded. This brought its own excitement, waiting to let her rip after the long haul with the brakes on. As soon as the headland comes abeam in situations like we were in, there is a temptation to bear off too early, which often results in the boat being blown back towards the headland in question. Having patience, born of experience, and going well forward in the sea, assures having plenty sea room to leeward after tacking. I had come across the situation many times before but these are the things I like to pass on to novice sailors when the opportunity presents itself.

As expected, we had good sailing when we rounded Bray Head. As we made for Dingle Harbour there was the feeling for me of having partaken in another significant seagoing adventure and when we tied up at Dingle Marina I felt the same sense of joy as I did on Glandore Pier seventeen years earlier when I docked *Eibhlís*. We had a welcoming party of family and friends at the marina. My crew and I then went to the Boatyard Restaurant and were treated to a meal on the house, courtesy of my niece Caroline (who is the chef there) and the management. We then retired to Tom's bar (McCarthy's) and told outlandish tales of seafaring on the high seas between Cornwall and Dingle.

Hayseed at mooring

A couple of days later I moved *Hayseed* to her permanent mooring at the western end of the harbour. While I was tidying up after the voyage I came across strawberry jam in the most unexpected places. During the course of the passage between Union Hall and Dingle, the Macroom bread and strawberry jam was a big hit with the crew. I found the jam on the logbook, the dividers and on the chart. Right smack in the middle of the gap between Dursey Island and the mainland a blob rendered all passage from north to south impossible. With a happy sigh I looked through the porthole at my surroundings and thought, 'It's good to be home'.

Eibhlís and Hayseed in Union Hall

Chapter 2

Hayseed is a Hit

The early summer of 2013 was much talked about during and after its arrival. The consistent sunshine gave everyone a lift. It brought out the best in people, though the outrageous shorts and other fine weather fashions on view were an insult to the eye and people didn't know where to stow their sunglasses: on the head, round the neck, hanging, etc. The torment must have been excruciating for the wearers. Barry and I went south to Union Hall during the thick of the heatwave and on the way *Hayseed* followed the tracks of her predecessors and was introduced to new coves and harbours along the way. After leaving Oileán Chléire on the third day of the trip, we sailed away south, availing of the fresh south-easterly breeze that materialised and tacked a few hours later to bring us to the entrance to Union Hall.

The parade of sail in Glandore was on that year but we did not enter, preferring to do our own thing on the day. I had the usual assortment of guests and crew for the event, apart from Barry, who I sold off the night before to a solo sailor named Fitzy who was shorthanded and disenchanted with the goings-on and was determined to chuck in the event. Barry gladly offered to help and, after an ignominious start beside the old pier, he and his 'new' skipper got going and enjoyed the day. On the following day Barry and I rowed out to *Hayseed* after lunching ashore and I was delighted to see *Eibhlís* moored next to *Hayseed* in the harbour.

The water was calm under a clear sky and the backdrop of greenery to the scene was remarkable. Barry took the photograph on which the sketch above is based. *Hayseed* appears to be standing back in reverence to *Eibhlís* and waiting for her to make the next move, as if saying: 'Where you go, I will follow.' Between them, both vessels have over one hundred years of sailing and tens of thousands of miles under their keels. Their past adventures and stories will never be fully told and I'm sure their futures will continue to give pleasure to all who come in contact with them.

Chapter 3

A Warm Welcome in Kinvara and Roundstone a First

Barry was back on board again as I sailed *Hayseed* north for the first time in mid-June of 2014. Catherine Twomey, who had sailed on *Eibhlís* in the past and had considerable sailing experience on various boats out of Fenit with Tralee Sailing Club, was also with us for the six days we spent along the Galway coast. An overnight sail from Dingle, on a course of 042 from Sybil Head, brought us through the sound between the island of Inisheer and the coast of Clare soon after midnight. Two hours later we had Black Head abeam to starboard and set a course east along Galway Bay for the entrance to Kinvara. We dropped anchor off Bush Pier, at the north-western end of Kinvara Bay, at 0540. We had covered the distance from Dingle Harbour in seventeen hours, ten minutes. In a sea dotted with jellyfish, we settled down for a well-deserved sleep. On the way north, though watches were assigned, we were all anxious to experience the fine calm night and pick out lights of lighthouses along the way: Loop Head, Inisheer light, etc.

At 1100 hours, Barry cooked a breakfast of bacon, eggs and fried banana. We rowed to the pier, well rested and eager to explore, and there we met a kind gentleman who gave us a lift to the village, which was about three miles by road. The day was warm and the weather was showing signs of settling into a fine spell. The summer growth, with its pleasant fragrances, was abundant along the roadside. Our informative taxi man dropped us off at the pier in Kinvara where we went to the Tide Full Inn and had excellent coffee and cakes, followed by an early (five o'clock) wine. There we relaxed and took stock of our surroundings. Sitting out in the sunshine, we savoured the time. Several other tourists had the same idea.

I phoned a good friend, Maura (O'Keeffe) Mulligan, who lives in the area and she came by and drove us back to her home, where we freshened up and enjoyed the hospitality of the Mulligan family. Patrick, Maura's husband, and their son Donal were present, as was Maura's sister, Fionnula, and their niece Sarah. My crew and I spent a nice couple of hours in the house beside the old Doorus Mill. Donal gave a guided tour of the mill and explained its history to Barry and Catherine. We had a glass of wine on the rear patio and Maura, who is a renowned fiddle player, gave Barry, who had recently taken up the same instrument, some introductory lessons. I was keen to see that Barry became proficient on the fiddle as I didn't want us both to end up in a Holmes-and-Watson situation aboard the boat whereby he (Barry) tore at the strings and I (his Watson) cowered at every stroke. Maura, please be thorough, I thought. We dined later at the Pier Head, where we were served excellent meals of duck, mussels and chicken by an affable waiter named Harvey. Then we went to Patrick's local, The Travellers Inn, to round off a very enjoyable evening. We walked back to our dinghy at a respectable hour and Catherine broke into song – a somewhat humorous and mischievous ditty called the 'Gay Cavelero' – before lights out.

The long haul west along Galway Bay began the next day after a breakfast of (very hard) boiled eggs and toast. Our destination was Roundstone. The wind was tight on the foresail so we motor-sailed most of the way. Barry plotted the course again, which brought us on 280° to Letermullen. The coast of Connemara is strewn with rocks and stones which, in hairy weather, would have the heart crossways in any decent sailor, but our day was fair with good visibility and we passed the time identifying and marking the myriad rocks and small islands along the way. Catherine had brought along a respectable Italian red and at five o'clock in the afternoon we celebrated our progress thus far with a glass of wine each. The five o'clock wine (one only) became a pleasant adjunct to our dietary regime during the cruise. Catherine was fitting in well and enjoyed the banter between Barry and me. She had a humorous streak of her own, which put us both in our place with subtle aplomb when activated. Our group was an easy and amicable trio in the comfortable surroundings of the good ship *Hayseed*. We each fell to our tasks, with honest intent for the betterment of the voyage – just as it should be. After Letermullen we made into the inner passage leaving scores of rocks and small islands to port. When we got to Macdaras Island we went on 016° to Roundstone Harbour.

We dropped anchor at 2215 off Roundstone Pier and set the table for a welcome meal of chicken kebabs and assorted vegetables. After a good night's sleep; early the next morning we launched the dinghy and set about exploring the village, which was high up from the level of the harbour. A generous breakfast in Ryan's Café, where the Wi-Fi code was 'buy a cup of coffee', went down well and set us up for the day. The village was busy with tourists like ourselves and an air of contentment abounded, which presumably had a lot to do with the agreeable weather that had kick-started the summer. Souvenirs were bought and a few of the local craft beers were sampled. Barry and I inspected the old pier where I came across a fishing boat that I had a hand in building while serving my apprenticeship in Dingle Boatyard very many moons ago.

Roundstone anchorage

After a couple of hours ashore we returned to *Hayseed* and made ready for the southward run towards home. Alas, Killary was not on the agenda this time round because of time constraints. A pleasant five-hour sail, south and then south-east, with a fair wind had *Hayseed* in Kilronan at 2200. We tied outside a fishing boat. We ate on board and went ashore for a while where we got a bottle of wine (for the next five o'clock) at cost price in Tí Joe Watty's. On returning to the boat we found that a kind fisherman had left some crabs claws in a bucket for us. They were immediately potted, cooked and consumed in the cockpit between verses of song, which were carried over the water in the still night only to bounce off the concrete walls and piers of the harbour and make their way back to us again. The echo was amazing and gave the impression that sailors in other boats were participating in our early morning revelry.

At 0300 we decided to begin the southward sail home; we passed through the Gregory Sound thirty minutes later and set course for the Blasket Sound. A gentle north-easterly drove us along and at 1600 hours we had Sybil Head abeam and the majestic Blaskets to starboard, basking under warm sunshine. Three hours later, my crew and I had our feet under the table in my home where my ever reliable home crew had a meal of salmon, chicken and roast vegetables prepared for the hungry sailors.

Chapter 4

Going inside the Puffin and Farewell for Now

In early September of 2014, *Hayseed* sailed south on a mini voyage with me, Barry and Tom McCarthy on board. We were availing of the extended summer weather that would last for the whole of that month. After we rounded Bray Head, making for Portmagee, we encountered a huge swell which carried swathes of foam in its troughs and peaks. I had never seen the foam in such prolific amounts before. It was obviously being bounced back to the sea from cliffs after they had been pummelled by the swell, which was probably a leftover from a deep low pressure area that had travelled north out in the Atlantic a few days before. Guinness, a company famous for its TV adverts, one of which features a surf-boarder atop the agitated froth of a pint glass, missed a huge opportunity to film three sailors ploughing through the sea of froth. There was no significant wind under the clear sky – just a big rolling sea tossing us hither and thither.

There was a free berth at the newly opened pontoon at Portmagee, where we tied up for the night. After Tom had scrubbed and scraped the neglected boat's tender, we had a good meal ashore after which we undertook an inspection of the fishing pier and its goings-on. Following an obligatory visit to the Fisherman's Inn for a chat with the locals, we retired with the anticipation of Barry's cooked breakfast in our thoughts.

At midday the next day we set south again for Sneem in the Kenmare River. The frothy sea and the swell were still there. Again the wind was negligible. The hoisted mainsail kept us steady in the lumpy sea. Puffin Island was ahead of us and I suggested to my crew that we go through the gap between the island and the mainland. I had not navigated the sound before and anytime I passed to seaward of the island, I was curious as to what lay on the other side.

The middle of the sound is strewn with rocks and as we approached we could not distinguish the breaking water from the foam that was predominant in the vicinity. I was using a handheld GPS (and would not have tried the stunt without it), from which I determined that there was a clear gap of about forty metres between the middle rocks and the island. Trepidation mounted as we got nearer. The wash from the mainland and the island intensified the foam to the extent that there was white water across the whole gap before us.

There was a bit of devilment in our challenge and, like similar undertakings where fate is being tempted, there comes a point of no return after which turning back is no longer an option. The crew, of course, were leaving the matter in my hands and probably harboured doubts along the lines of 'What's he up to now?' Barry was up front looking out for hidden dangers and Tom was behind me and may have been saying the rosary. Onward into the breach, as it were, and I knew exactly when there was no turning back. For the next couple of minutes after that, the ride was exhilarating. On exiting south of the sound there was a collective sigh, followed by a loud 'yippee ki-yay'.

Soon after clearing the island the foam disappeared. Bolus Head was to the south-east and when we were abeam of it we rounded and plotted a course that would take us north of Scariff and Deenish Islands. At Lamb's Head, which marks the northern entrance into the Kenmare River, we put *Hayseed* on a course of 070°, which brought us south of Sherky Island. From there we rounded north and headed for Sneem Harbour.

The anchorage at the mouth of the Sneem Estuary was calm and surrounded by profuse greenery from low-lying shrubbery and tall trees. The scene was postcard-like and the smell of sea and fruity growth was pleasing to the senses. We launched the dinghy and paddled ashore to a slipway at Oysterbed Pier. From there we had a three-mile walk into the village of Sneem where our first order of business was to find a good eating house. At The Blue Bull, we managed to get our order in before last call. The food was very good and the staff welcoming. Walking around the village later, we came across an unusual display of permanent weather-proof signs hanging from poles in a small park; they had photos of local people with attached commentaries about their lot in life and the financial challenges they were facing during the downturn in the economy. It was ordinary people having their say in public in a very original way.

On the sail back to Dingle the next day, I was in the bad books with the crew as I had forgotten to get a replacement gas cylinder – and the peculiar thing was that it was the same crew that found me wanting when the same thing happened a year previously. We endured a coffee-less eight hours on the way north, this time staying outside (west of) the Puffin.

As I conclude, it seems a long time since I first sailed south with Fr Gearoid. This written account seems meagre compared with the many hours I have spent at sea over thirty summers. There have been several other voyages I have omitted in order to avoid duplication and consequently not all who crewed with me are mentioned in these pages. I have learned from all who sailed with me and I hope that the extended crew who have spent time on board with me took something away from the experience. I like to see crew members return for a second or third trip. That way I know that things are OK under my captaincy. While it's the voyage and not the destination that counts, I must confess that I do enjoy arriving as well and meeting the people and characters at the other end.

In the modern age we live in I am regularly amused by new-fangled curative options for people who have issues with everyday living: anger management courses and empathic therapy have become psychological crutches for many. I believe that sailing provides much in the way of therapy for many ills. Sail-training on larger ships especially engenders discipline and community co-operation between the participants. As I look forward to sailing on *Hayseed* in the future, I wish for the same good fortune I have been blessed with until now: that I will never be short of crew; that the people I meet onshore will be welcoming; and above all that the sea will continue to treat me kindly.

***

I hoist the main while still tied to the mooring. The southerly wind off the land on the southern shore is brisk and waiting for gainful employment. I unhook from the mooring, haul in the boom and point at the lighthouse to the east. *Hayseed* heels gently towards the north. The unfurled foresail adds a knot or two and I am on my way. The foliage on the hill to my right is full with shades of green and amber growth. Birds flutter about a farmer who is tending his patch. A half-decker passes to port under a flock of erratically swooping gulls that fight for the discarded innards from the deckhands busily gutting their catch. At the harbour's mouth the dolphin entertains the tourists. I make a path through the ferry boats and I am into the bay.

The sea is shimmering in the wind and sparkles of sunshine are mirrored in its gently rolling expanse. I am hauled in tight on a south-easterly course making ground enough before I tack for the Blasket Islands to the west. I am alone. It is the first sail of the season, on a late May day. Well south now I make the tack and leave the south shore to port. Kells Harbour is behind my left shoulder and the islands beckon. As I go west along the bay, I see the landmarks on the cliff architecture of the seaward side of Burnham Hill: the Clothes Iron, the Ball Alley and, on top, Eask Tower, where my father spent the war years in the coast-watching service. I never go into the bay without thinking of my paternal ancestors who fished from Nobbies in the Age of Sail. With the entrance to Ventry abeam I look around and see that the bay is all mine. The small boat's radio is my only contact with the larger world. At Slea Head a school of porpoises does a criss-crossing dance off the bow. The southerly stiffens as I head for the white beach on the Blascaod Mór. It too is devoid of any human presence. As I near the island, I see the waves break into froth on the undisturbed sand. I ease off the sails and head north on the road through the sound. It is two hours since I left my mooring.

Hayseed under sail

After clearing Beginish and the Edge Rocks I turn west on a beam-reach for Inishtooskert. This will bring me into open water. The air is fresh and full of the scent of the sea. On my face I can feel the foundation of my summer patina being laid. Whisks of salt spray make it back to the cockpit as I tighten the sheets for a south-westerly course towards Inishtearaght, the westernmost island. I am now on a middle path between the northern side of the Blascaod Mór and the islands Inishtearaght and Inishtooskert. *Hayseed* is cutting through the churned-up water. I continue till my beam is well beyond the gap between Canduff (the western end of the Blascaod Mór) and Inisnabro. My plan is to tack and make for the gap and exit at the southern side of the island group. The going is exhilarating, the scenery incomparable and again it is all mine.

Thinking I am well positioned, I go about and make for the mile-wide gap borne by the fresh southerly which is at 45° to my track. I am flying, sitting on the high side. From down below I hear the clatter of cups and cutlery and it is music to my ears. The foredeck is getting a salt scrub and my cheeks are stinging from slivers of sea blown back. The only other place I would rather be is aloft looking down on *Hayseed's* progress cutting a frothy path through the waves. I gain on the opening in a short time and soon have the spectacular Inishnabro to starboard. Well clear, I slack off sail and head along the southern side of the Blascaod Mór. Inishvickillane is way astern; on a beam reach again I am doing seven knots. I head for Slea Head and home, now in the company of a large fishing boat returning from the deep. Across the bay Valentia Island looks inviting. Bray Head and its possibilities tease my roving inclinations, but that will wait for another day.

The evening sun is still ablaze as I pass Dingle Lighthouse. The wind off the hill is waiting for my return. I sail parallel with the shore to my mooring and hook up. I tidy my boat and board the dinghy and row off. After a while I stop and look back at *Hayseed* afloat at her tackle and the day she gave me replays in my mind. I turn for home and start planning my next voyage.

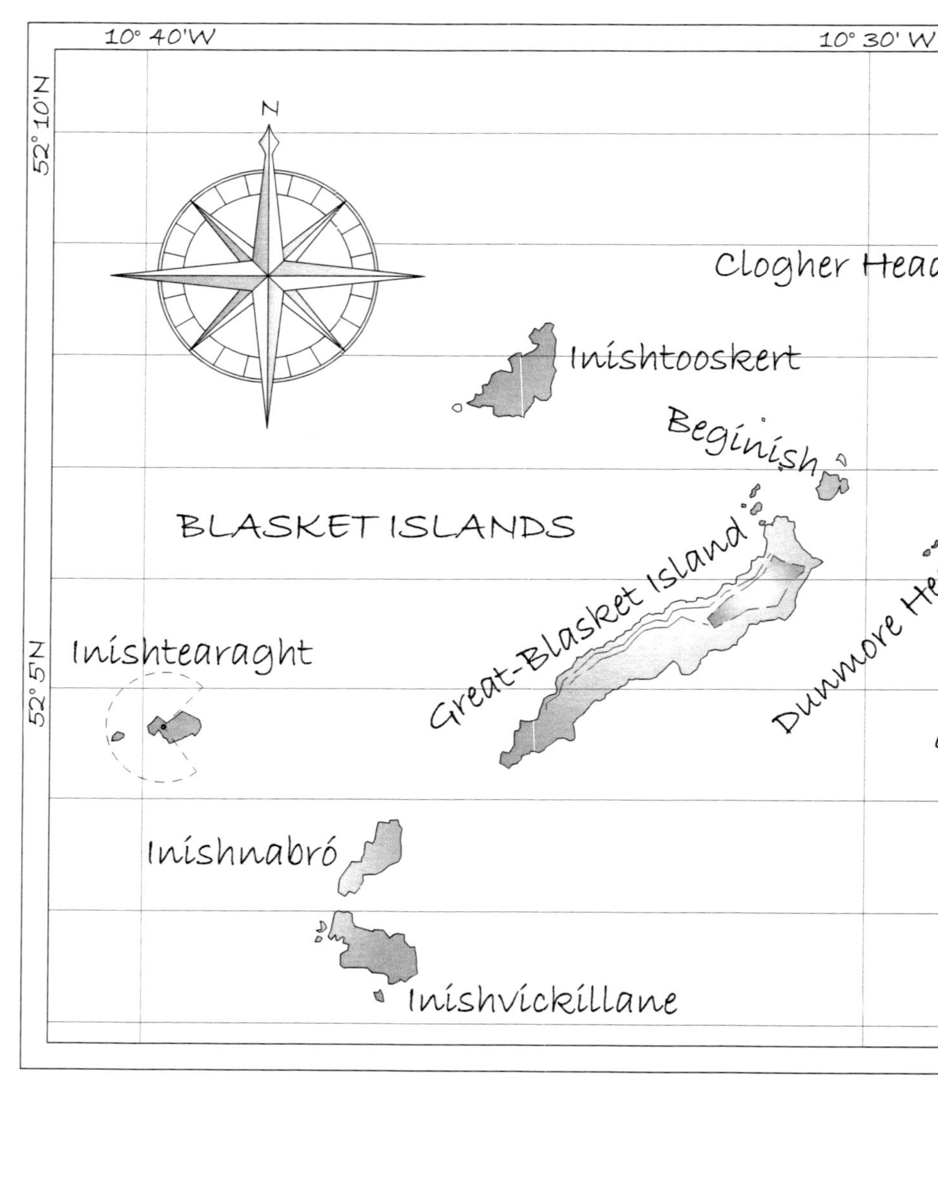
10° 40'W
10° 30' W
52° 10'N
52° 5'N
N
Clogher Head
Inishtooskert
Beginish
BLASKET ISLANDS
Great-Blasket Island
Dunmore He
Inishtearaght
Inishnabró
Inishvickillane

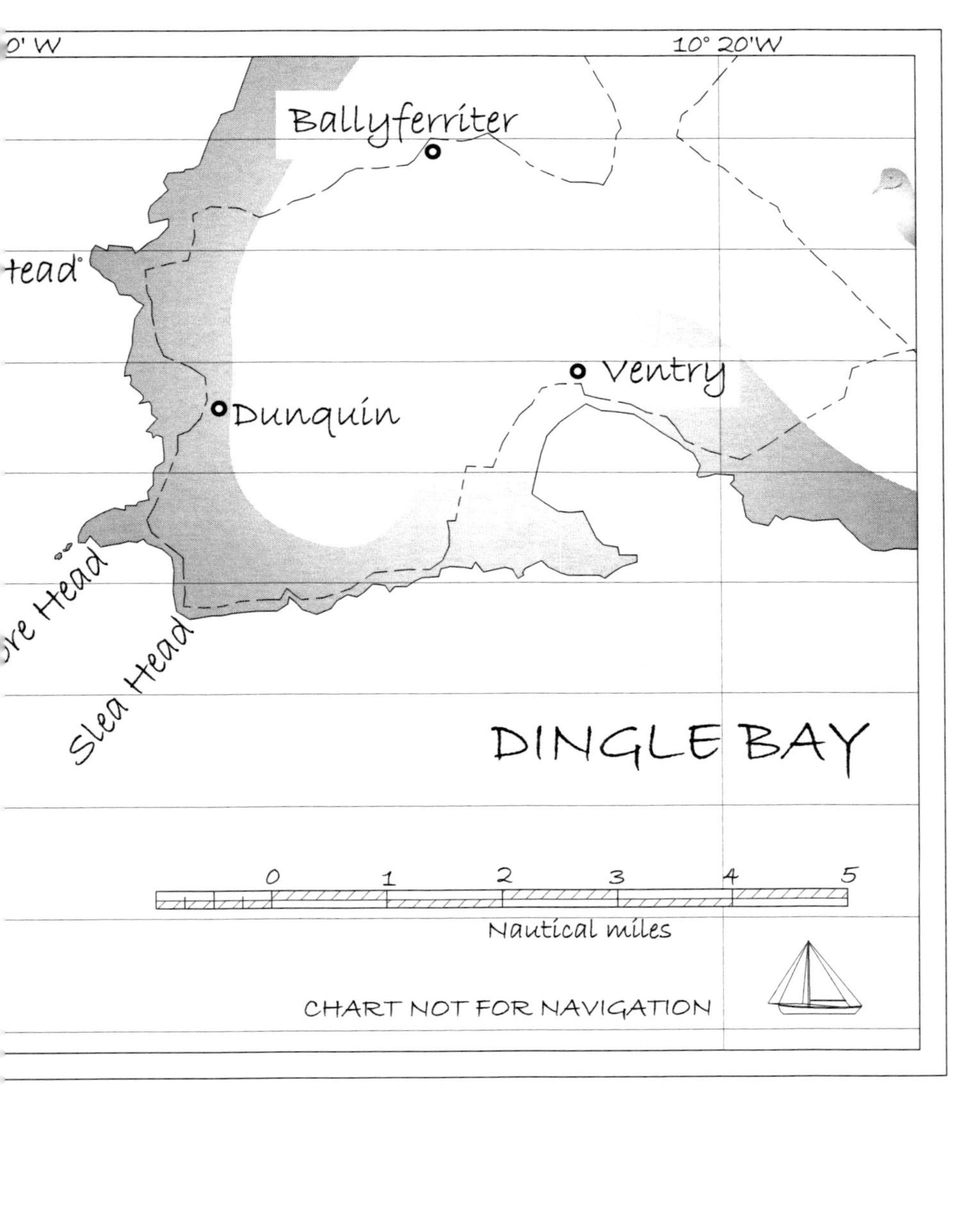

0' W
10° 20'W
Ballyferriter
Head
Dunquin
Ventry
re Head
Slea Head
DINGLE BAY
0
1
2
3
4
5
Nautical miles
CHART NOT FOR NAVIGATION